# CHOICES

*One mother's determined search for the supports to meet the needs of her aging autistic son.*

## J M CRAWFORD

This book is a memoir. The author has attempted to recreate events, locales and conversations from her memories of them and saved correspondence. The opinions expressed within this book are solely her own. The author does not assume and hereby disclaims any liability to any party for any loss, damage, or disruption caused by errors or omissions, whether such errors or omissions result from negligence, accident, or any other cause.

Copyright © 2019 by Johanne Kieffer

Crawford, J.M.

Choices: One mother's determined search for the supports to meet the needs of her aging Autistic son / J.M. Crawford

*Summary:* A mother lives through the joys and sorrows of raising an autistic child and finds the courage and determination to navigate her way through red tape and roadblocks to find the help he needs as he enters adulthood.

ISBN: 978-1-7329898-0-1

Swing High Press
P.O. Box 1127
403 South Orleans Road
Orleans, MA 02662


Published in the United States of America

*For Ian and all those like him who cannot speak for themselves, whose lives depend on the choices of others.*

*And for all the families who navigate this journey of uncertainty, may your voices always be heard. Remember, you always have a choice.*

# DISCLAIMER

This book is based on a true story as seen through the eyes of the author. All names (people and day habilitation facilities) have been changed with the exception of the author, her son, Barnert Memorial Hospital, Elizabeth Warren and Barack Obama.

*Part One*

# CHANCES

"*Make the best use of what's in your power
and take the rest as it happens.*"
-Epictetus

# FATE

It was unusually quiet for a late Friday afternoon, but I knew the hush wouldn't last. In fifteen minutes the clock would strike five and I would be surrounded by people vying for a space on the busy highway. The long row of parked vehicles looked like the auto mall. Finally, I spotted my silver Tercel among the SAABS, BMWs and Japanese sports cars I could not yet afford. As I opened the car door, a large gold Cadillac came to a stop beside me. The electric passenger window slowly opened. *Everybody always gets lost around here, I'm sure he wants directions*, I thought as I approached the car. I was about two feet from it and could see into the front seat. "Get in the car!" he demanded. Simultaneously, he lifted a gun from the passenger front seat and pointed it at me.

My mind couldn't connect what I was seeing and hearing. I felt like a bystander observing the scene. "Get outta here!" flew out of my mouth, a typical Jersey response accompanied by the wave and attitude that goes along with it, like Robert De Niro in the movie *Taxi Driver* when he says, "You talkin to me?" I turned and started powerwalking back toward the office building, then quickly broke into a trot. Before I hit the bottom of the steps I turned around to see if I could read the license plate. He drove away slowly, but he was too far from where I stood to read the plate.

Inside, I reported what had just happened to the security desk. Wandering back to my office, I noticed Ted was still at his desk, in his office adjacent to mine. I slipped in and quietly placed myself in the chair before him. "You're not going to believe what just happened," I said. "Some guy just held me up with a gun." No further explanation was needed. Within minutes, uniformed police officers stampeded down the hallway, followed by a rush of plain clothes undercover cops. It was like watching a movie. One plain clothes cop caught my eye; he stood out from the rest. *He's cute*, I thought.

He was dressed in sneakers, jeans, a T-shirt and an oversized suit jacket with rolled up sleeves. His hair was two contrasting shades of blonde with a braided two-inch 'tail' down the back of his neck. Tails were in style then. He looked like an 80's rock star, the only thing missing, a pierced ear. Clearly this was a pleasant distraction, though on the surface, we couldn't have appeared more opposite. The police told me to report directly to headquarters to make an official statement. My friend and coworker, Arietta, insisted she would escort me. This was not the evening Ari and I had planned. We were supposed to attend a fundraiser at the Hilton. Back out into the parking lot once more, Ari and I walked toward her car. We passed my Tercel and the car door was still open, a snapshot of the aftermath of fleeing so quickly from the attempted abduction. It was difficult to wrap my head around it; this was in fact a crime scene. I stopped, checked out the car, and locked the door. Silently, we sat as Ari drove across the highway into the heart of downtown to police headquarters.

The undercover cop with the braided tail was seated behind a large wooden desk with an old manual typewriter in front of him. I sat down across from him in a small metal chair. He asked me to explain what had happened and I began telling the tale. My words were accompanied by the clicking sounds of his hunt-and-peck typing. I stated time, place, what I was doing and what I had seen, describing the driver as "... a young black man, clean-cut, short hair, with chubby cheeks. He looked like someone who would work in our customer service department," I said, reporting every detail I could.

The last key stroke and the sound of paper being ripped from the carriage signaled the statement was complete. He walked around the desk and asked me to read the freshly typed paper and sign it if everything was correct, an easy task for a well-seasoned proofreader. I had been proofreading copy since my high school days in secretarial class. As I scanned the text, I noticed he typed "cubby" instead of "chubby" describing the driver's cheeks. All I could think of was the Mouseketeers Roll Call: *Cubby! Annette!*

*What's wrong with me?*

I'm in the middle of giving a police statement about an attempted abduction and all I can think of is the Mouseketeers.

"You have a typo here," I said pointing to the error. He sat down next to me and in a quiet voice with his North Jersey accent said, "I don't wanna scare you honey, but this was an attempted abduction."

*No shit, Sherlock! Did he think I was an idiot?*

He brought me some mug shots, 3"x5" photo albums filled with faces of men who had broken the law. I looked at each one carefully, then handed them back. "I don't see him." I looked at my watch and complained, "I'm going to be late."

"We're done," he said. "Late to where?"

I told him about the fundraiser at the local Hilton, complaining I still had to run home and change.

"The Hilton? That's my watering hole," he said. "Maybe I'll see you there later." He smiled and escorted me out to the entrance, where Ari had been waiting.

We left the building and she drove me back to my car. What just happened? *Was that guy hitting on me?* I kept my thoughts to myself.

"Are you okay?" Ari asked.

"Yeah", I replied, "just wanna get home and change, I'm okay." She pulled up next to my car and I got out.

"I'll see you back at the Hilton." I slid into the driver seat, turned the key and pulled onto the highway; my car seemed to know the way home. What I had experienced only a couple of hours ago did not yet register. After a quick change of clothes, a la Clark Kent, I was back on the road in a flash. Off to the Hilton for a night of fun and, dare I say, excitement. Hadn't there been enough of that already?

The Hilton was packed. I squeezed through the crowd and scanned the sea of bobbing heads, looking for Ari. Finally spotting her, I waved. "Ari, over here!" I yelled above the noise. We moved toward each other and headed into the room where the fundraiser was taking place. On stage, attractive men and women paraded like models down the runway while the auctioneer set a starting bid for a date. It was all good fun for a good cause. The bidding wars were too pricy for either of us, but it was fun to watch and we had done our small part by just purchasing tickets. Thirty minutes of that was plenty for Ari and me. It was time to move into the lounge by the bar. The dance floor was small, but fully equipped with a disco ball, strobe lights and music so loud it pulsated in my chest. We stayed on the outer fringe of the crowd and I attempted conversation above the fever pitch nightclub energy, but Ari kept looking at me with an odd expression. Finally, she timidly pointed behind me and I turned around. It was him, the one with the braided tail, the officer who had taken my statement a few hours earlier.

He smiled and said, "Hi, can I buy you a drink?"

This was the second surprise of the day. Suddenly I was a bit nervous. He asked Ari if she would like one as well, but she declined. He left to get our drinks.

Ari leaned over with a sly smile. "I'm gonna circulate, I'll catch up with you later," she said and promptly disappeared into the crowd.

The cop bore a striking resemblance to the actor Michael Douglas, I thought, the blue-eyed sandy-blonde actor who played an undercover cop in the 1970's television series *The Streets of San Francisco*. He handed me the drink with a genuine look in his eyes and a friendly smile on his face. He stepped into my personal space. "I'm Doug, by the way."

In that moment, I felt a visceral surge, a lightning-bolt attraction. This didn't happen at headquarters, what was different?

It didn't occur to me until later, but at the Hilton he was not "on the job" as the cop lingo goes, he was just another Joe. The person now before me was human, real. I felt that vibration to my core.

# FAMILY

*L*ike many of my former colleagues, I found myself collecting unemployment after a major company buyout and reorganization in the last days of 1989. The chain reaction that followed was a personal budget review and job search, my new business of the day. It was clear I could no longer afford my apartment and would have to relocate, but where? My father and his siblings had recently inherited my grandmother's house and it was now vacant, an ideal opportunity for me to rent at a rate I could afford while they decided what to do with it.

I moved in and began looking for work. Time after time I would come up empty on job offers; over-qualified for one position, underqualified for the next. It was like spitting into the wind. I finally gave in to an offer made by the very corporation that axed my entire department in the takeover. I swallowed my pride, took a salary cut and accepted the position. It felt like surrendering to the enemy, but it paid the rent. Many of the employees were familiar faces, employees who stayed put after the buyout. This cushioned the ego blow we all had to take on some level. I moved forward as usual and earned my keep.

My family spent many Sundays and holidays within the walls of my grandmother's house. A small, white, Cape Cod style home located on a quiet street, sandwiched between neighboring houses bordered by a front concrete sidewalk, a streetlight planted directly across the road. In the center of the postage-stamp front lawn, the American flag flew from a flagpole. Both my grandmother and her second husband were immigrants, she from Ireland and he from Sweden. The flag stood as a symbol of gratitude for the new life they found in America.

The overgrown dogwood tree in the backyard had generations of tales to tell of the children who played and climbed on its branches. The familiar town park was a short walk around the corner, the supermarket within walking distance, and Main Street a five-minute drive. You could catch the Amtrak train in the next town over or take a ten-minute drive to the nearest major highway leading right into NYC. You could work in the city and live in the suburbs, a commuter's dream location.

Doug and I had been back and forth to each other's apartments so frequently over the next fourteen months we were practically living together. Eventually, he moved out of his apartment to live with me. We slipped into typical suburban life, deciding we would marry before the end of the year. That summer, he surprised me with a cruise to Bermuda for my 35th birthday. By August, I had a surprise for him; I was pregnant. We had tossed fate to wind. No birth control for us. We were getting married and wanted children, but who knew it would happen so quickly? Suddenly setting a wedding date was front and center.

In September we were married at town hall in the presence of my parents, Ari, my brother and his wife. A simple celebratory dinner followed at a local restaurant with some wedding cake back at the house. A couple of photos were snapped for a small album. No honeymoon. Back to work on Monday.

Doug already had one child from his second marriage, a boy; his name was Doug, too. He was six years old and came regularly to visit with his dad. He was a friendly kid and called me "Jo." One sunny afternoon, we decided to have an old-fashioned picnic outside. "Little Dougy," as we often called him, lived on the second floor in a condo across the river from the busy city of Manhattan on the Jersey side. He didn't have a yard and the idea of a real picnic on a blanket, outside on the ground, excited him. We spread the blanket and laid out the picnic feast. Halfway through lunch, I felt something wet on my thigh. I excused myself and quickly headed for the house.

By the time I reached the bathroom, there was blood streaming down my leg. I quickly undressed and grabbed some tissue to wipe it clean. More had dropped into the toilet, it looked like a lot. I cringed in fear I had lost our baby; I was two months pregnant. I took a breath, cleaned up, changed my clothes and called the doctor; she saw me the next day. I lay silently on the examining table feeling the cold gel on my belly. She dragged the ultrasound probe across my abdomen and carefully watched the computer monitor. Pointing to the fuzzy gray and black image on the screen, she told me there was only a twenty percent chance this would develop into a full-term baby. I was both crushed and in disbelief. *See it through and let nature take its course*, I heard in my head, so I followed my intuition.

The pregnancy continued. At four months, I knew what came next, an amniocentesis. This test is strongly recommended to pregnant women age 35 or older, to rule out chromosome defects and developmental abnormalities in the growing fetus. It is also risky and can trigger a spontaneous abortion. My brush with miscarriage only two months earlier flashed in my mind's eye. Reluctantly, I

11

signed the consent form, believing that was in the best interest of our unborn baby.

Doug and I exhaled when the test came back unremarkable. "Do you want to know the baby's sex?" asked the nurse. "Yes," we responded in unison. "It's a girl," she said. We decided to call her Marianne. As the months passed, I talked to her and called her by name. Toward the final weeks of my pregnancy, I traveled to the local teaching hospital to check on the baby's vital signs twice a week. Approaching the 42$^{nd}$ week of my pregnancy, there were still no signs of labor. My final visit revealed there was little fluid in my amniotic sac. Unbeknownst to me, I had a slow leak; there was a tear in the sac. I was quickly becoming dry as a bone.

"That baby needs to be delivered now," the young female resident barked at me.

"I'm supposed to have my baby at Barnert Memorial Hospital, not here," I said.

"Sign yourself out then. How do I know you're not going to the mall?" she barked again.

I was in tears. The nurse at the entrance desk compassionately offered assistance. In a world long before cell phones, beepers were the cutting edge in communication technology. The nurse beeped my doctor and my husband.

Fighting to see through the tears, I jumped in my car and drove ten miles down the road, arriving at the emergency entrance to the hospital alone. I was immediately admitted. My doctor and Doug arrived shortly thereafter, around 5 p.m. I still had not dilated so they induced labor with Pitocin. My body was connected to wire electrodes to monitor the contractions. With each contraction a jagged image appeared, like a mountain drawn on the screen. Doug was sprawled out in a chair dozing on and off almost in sync with my contractions. Still no dilation.

The doctor ordered Doug to leave the room. She then told me she was going to break my water, or what was left of it. Still no change. If I did not dilate by 6 a.m. she was going to perform a caesarian section; that baby had to be delivered.

Doug returned to the room and stayed with me throughout the night, planted on the hospital chair at the foot of my bed as CNN played in the background. I was no more dilated at 6 a.m. than I was at 5 p.m. the day before. I was prepped for surgery. I did not want a spinal, I was too nervous. I feared I would never last through the procedure and would surely jump off the table. The anesthesiologist administered general. Everything went blank.

In recovery under the drug-induced fog, I slowly pried my eyes open, seeing through blurry vision an oxygen mask on my face. Doug was by my side. Tears flowed down his cheeks as he held up the ink footprints of our new baby girl. I felt nauseous, paralyzed by the drugs. I feared I would vomit in my oxygen mask and choke. I mustered up every ounce of strength in my body and with one swipe of my hand successfully removed the mask.

The nurse promptly came across the room and placed it back over my face. I was doomed, convinced I was going to die from choking on my own vomit. I blacked out again. They moved me to a room where I remained hospital-bound for about a week. I had a reaction to one of the medications and my body swelled up like a balloon; even my feet were swollen. I couldn't lift my head off the pillow for three days. I still hadn't held my newborn.

Finally, after what seemed like months I could sit up and begin to eat. Every move felt like a bear trap squeezing my abdomen. They used staples to close my C-section incision. It was excruciating just to walk several feet to the bathroom and back while tears streamed down my face from the pain. Still hooked up to the I.V., I dragged it with me like a ball and chain. What had I done to deserve this? I gingerly got myself back into bed and heard a baby crying. The cries got louder and louder. A nurse entered my room.

"Someone's hungry," I said.

"That's your baby!" the nurse replied. "Can I bring her in for a feeding?"

I nodded. As the nurse walked into the room cradling my new baby girl in her arms, in my best sing-song voice I said, "Marianne, come to mommy."

"Did you see that? She turned her head when you called her by name," exclaimed the nurse.

"Well, I've been talking to her for nine months," I replied.

"No, she knows her name." The nurse went on to tell me about studies done on moms who talk to their babies while they are still in the womb; they can hear you. She gently transferred Marianne from her arms to mine.

This was the first time I held her. Connected to me for all those months through the lifeline of the umbilical cord, we were reunited as separate beings. Tears of joy flowed down my face. This six-and-a-half-pound bundle with big blue eyes and strawberry-blonde hair was now looking back at me, a sight for sore eyes.

That 20% chance the doctor spoke about only months ago was born into this world in April 1991. Not long after that first meeting Doug, Marianne and I returned to the suburbs, now a family of three.

The last ten years my life before Marianne arrived consisted of fighting the morning commute, performing the daily grind, and cocktail business lunches while pursuing my bachelor's degree two nights a week; a typical "type A" personality. I was used to being in overdrive and running full tilt. Suddenly, it all came to a dramatic halt. In the blink of an eye, I was bound to the responsibility for another life. The first two weeks I was home from the hospital, I had to keep reminding myself there was a baby in the next room. One time, I was at the front door of the house with my hand on the doorknob, headed out to the store when the voice in my head reminded me, *You're a mom now.* How do you forget that?

To say the transition to motherhood was challenging is an

understatement. At age 36 I entered the mommy zone much older than most young mothers and with little experience. My life beyond that front door had changed forever. I had to reemerge with a new identity, one that had not yet formed.

Doug, on the other hand, had a seamless transition. He continued his career as a detective sergeant; his new baby girl was a feather in his cap, another accolade. I immersed myself in bonding with this vulnerable new life, fumbling through the days of motherhood not knowing quite what I was doing. I wanted everything to be right, to be as natural and environmentally friendly as possible for Marianne. She was fragile and new to this earth and my instinct to protect her was fierce. I breastfed, gave her organic baby food long before it was all the rage and used special Velcro rubber pants and cloth diapers; no Pampers for this child.

Everywhere I went, she went and like most new moms I took a gazillion photos. In the 1990's, all photos had to be developed at the local drug store, so you had to wait to see if the pictures actually turned out. Snapshots were always followed by the never-ending series of shopping mall photos: the Christmas photo, Easter photo and numerous "as she grows" photos. It was a scam, but most moms were hooked with "they're only small once," which meant you needed to capture every moment on film. In spite of knowing my own family photos ended up in the basement, on shelves in shoe boxes collecting dust, the guilt still won out and I paid for the photos anyway.

Now we lived as a family of three. I traded cocktail lunches for breastfeeding schedules; business trips for short jaunts to the market and the pediatrician. I had no regrets. A page had turned, a new chapter begun.

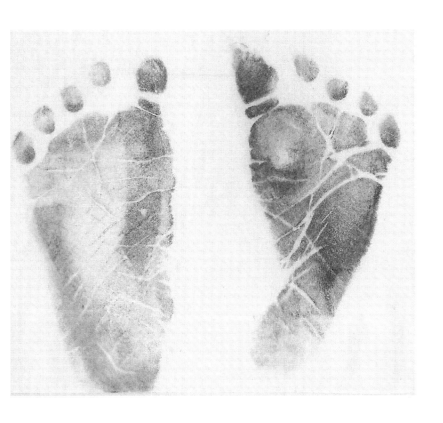

Our daughter's footprints, 1991

# HOPE

*W*e rented a cottage on Martha's Vineyard in the summer of 1992. Marianne was one year old and we were on our first real family vacation. Doug and I both loved the Vineyard and dreamed of retiring there someday, vowing if we didn't hit the lottery by then, we would happily settle into retirement on Cape Cod. As summer turned to the beginning of fall, I found out I was two months pregnant with our second child.

During a routine exam, the doctor discovered a lump in my right breast; it did not show up on a mammogram taken earlier that year. Since I was pregnant, another mammogram was out of the question. An ultrasound performed in the hospital revealed a dark, raisin-sized mark, a growth. My mother had been diagnosed with breast cancer only a decade ago. She was a survivor. Was I next?

The family medical history was complicated by my pregnancy. The doctor scheduled outpatient surgery the following week. With Marianne in tow, Doug brought me to the hospital for the procedure. I kissed them both goodbye. I'm not sure if they waited outside. I was scared, for me, the baby growing inside me and the one I'd just kissed goodbye. The procedure was to take about 45 minutes.

My nurse was a kind man with a long dark ponytail and soothing voice. Because of the pregnancy, I had local anesthesia and had to be awake for the entire procedure. The nurse kindly held my hand, offering comfort. As he wheeled me into the operating room, I felt the temperature drop. The icy cold room gleamed with shiny chrome. They strapped both my arms down perpendicular to my body, like I was being crucified. My anxiety began to escalate. The doctor explained what was about to take place. He injected the local anesthetic into my right breast several times. My heart pounded faster with each injection. I squeezed my nurse's hand so hard I'm sure I cut off his circulation at some point.

After a few minutes the doctor pressed the tissue on my breast. "Can you feel this, or this? How about this?"

"No, just pressure," I replied.

He began the incision. I felt pressure, but no pain. I tried to focus elsewhere and use the Lamaze breathing technique I had learned a couple years earlier while pregnant with Marianne.

I saw my body reflected in a shiny metal disc hanging from the ceiling. I could see the doctor's hands operating. I was not interested in watching my breast being sliced and quickly looked away. By this time, I'm sure the poor nurse's fingers were blue.

"So, where do you like to go on vacation?" the surgeon asked.

*Was he kidding?*

"We just came back from Martha's Vineyard," I replied politely.

The doctor continued working while recounting his own experiences on the Vineyard. My ears could only hear "WA-WA-WA-WA," just like the teacher's voice in the *Charlie Brown* cartoons. The smell of burning flesh was in the air. *He must be using something like an electro surge*, I thought. I had been a dental assistant for several years and knew this technique of burning the tissue helps to coagulate the blood.

At last, the doctor holds up the freed tumor before my eyes. Hanging from his tweezers, it's the size of a small meatball. "Looks good to me, probably benign," he says. "I'll send it down to the lab for further testing. Results will take about a week."

I exhaled. I was grateful it was over as was the nurse. I was stitched back together and wheeled into recovery. Doug and Marianne were there to take me home. I had made it over the first hurdle. Now came the waiting.

All kinds of thoughts raced through my brain, all the "what if" scenarios. I did not want to breathe a word of this to anyone, not even my parents. I wanted to deal with this privately. Born under the astrological sign of Cancer, the crab, my true Cancerian self was emerging. I wanted to withdraw back into my shell and keep both claws out front to guard against intruders. So, I withdrew, and waited through one of the longest weeks of my life.

Finally, the word "benign" came through the telephone wire and tears of relief welled up in my eyes. In an instant, the slate was wiped clean. My life no longer hung in the balance, the mounting fear for the developing unborn child I carried was released. We had turned yet another corner and life was back on track.

The next seven months seemed to fly by as we immersed ourselves in the day-to-day scheduling of doctor appointments, meals and family time. All of it revolved around Doug's rotating shifts at work and moonlighting jobs. Time was tight, so it was valuable.

Before long, spring arrived and I was scheduled to deliver our son at 38 weeks. My doctor scheduled another C-section to avoid a potential repeat of complications I had experienced delivering Marianne. This time I knew what was coming. I was beyond nervous. In less than 24 hours my life and my unborn baby's life would be placed in the hands of a medical team. We had arranged for Marianne to be taken care of so Doug and I could be at the hospital before 6 a.m. We awoke before dawn and soldiered through our morning routine with little conversation. I grabbed my bag and headed for the car. Doug took the wheel and we were off.

He took a different route and I worried we'd be late. "Where are you going?" I questioned. "This isn't the way."

A full-blown argument over directions exploded. We spewed all of our pent-up nervous energy at each other, a demonstration of Newton's Third Law, "for every action there is an equal and opposite reaction." Although Doug would never admit it, I'm sure he was just as nervous as I was.

Taking back what little control I had, I insisted he drop me off at the emergency door and meet me inside. He complied without hesitation, probably secretly happy to get a break from my crazy-making. I checked myself in, was taken upstairs and prepared for surgery. Doug made it to the room before they wheeled me into the O.R., he gave me a kiss and held my hand, giving it a firm but gentle squeeze before he let go. The senseless arguing only minutes ago faded away and the focus now was on our son, another addition to the family.

Ian was born into this world at the end of March 1993. I went home only two days later, as compared with the complicated week I had spent in the hospital recovering from delivering Marianne. We arrived home with our new 6 ¾ pounds healthy baby boy, now a family of four. He was born under the astrological sign of Aries, the first sign in the zodiac, symbolizing new beginnings, in sync with the energy of Mother Nature birthing new life.

---

BY THE TIME both kids were toddlers I had incorporated regular walks around the block into our days. We bought a red wagon large enough to seat them both; my two toddlers happy passengers while I did all of the walking and pulling. Their baby-fine blonde hair looked like duck down blowing in the breeze created by whatever strength I had that day to pull them along. Although he was two years shy of his older sister, Ian was a big boy and passersby often asked if they were twins.

One day, as we passed the house on the corner owned by a nice elderly couple, I noticed they were having a garage sale. Curious, I stopped with the kids to look. To my surprise they had a swing set. The couple told me their grandson was too old for the swings now. The nuts and bolts were all in plastic sandwich bags placed alongside piles of aluminum pipes. The set was a bit worn, not perfect, but the twenty-dollar price tag was. The deal was sealed. I stuffed the baggies around the kids in the wagon. Proud of my purchase, I headed toward home managing to carry the pipes with one arm while keeping the kids in tow.

Arriving home, I plopped the pipes and baggies on the backyard grass and recruited my husband to help with the kids while I attempted to reconstruct this contraption. I had no idea what I was doing. I laid out all the pipes, nuts and bolts on the picnic table in order by size, shape and quantity and began to piecemeal it together. I was the handyman of the house, not Doug. Hanging a picture on the wall was a major event for him, involving measuring, marking, and utilizing the right hanger. But I would eyeball just about anything. Give me a hammer and a nail, show me where you want it and it's done. I even put in a small brick walkway on the side of the house without a plan; I just recalled watching my dad do it and winged it. Two hours later, on this hot sticky August day, a swing set emerged in our backyard; a place for the kids to play.

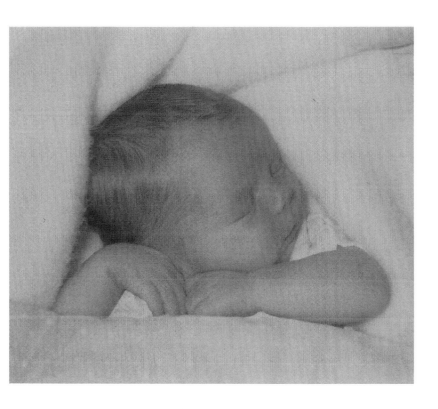

Newborn Ian, 1993

# BELOW THE SURFACE

*O*ur family was now complete; two parents, two kids and a dog, settled in our small home on a quiet street in the suburbs of New Jersey. Dad went to work; mom stayed home and took care of the kids. From the outside looking in, we were a Norman Rockwell family. This was my American dream, to be married and raise a family in a home with a white picket fence. Unbeknownst to me, Doug had a different perception.

The new year of 1994 brought a shift that I couldn't ignore, couldn't justify. Doug's habits around alcohol were increasingly changing. Any downtime now became an opportunity to drink. The simple task of mowing our postage stamp front lawn required a six-pack of beer. Any time off from work meant purchasing jugs of cheap wine and drinking most of the day while lying in the back-yard hammock. I had seen alcoholism on the fringe of family gatherings growing up. My grandmother's second husband and my uncle were both alcoholics. As I got older, my aunt and I developed a close relationship and she shared some of her personal stories with me. What was happening? Had I followed in their footsteps? Had I, too, married an alcoholic?

The signs were becoming clear. No sense in giving Doug a lecture on alcoholism; it would just incite anger and argument. How do I safely move through this? I had heard it said, "when you don't know what to do, do nothing." (Anonymous). So, I stood back, observed and kept close watch over my children.

In December of 1994, we were invited to the wedding of the son of one of Doug's friends on the police force. I asked my brother and his wife to babysit Ian and Marianne that day. The nuptials took place late afternoon, and the dreaded reception followed. Doug was his usual self, hanging at the bar, chatting away with a drink in one hand and a cigarette in the other. The next few hours consisted of the expected social graces while keeping an eye on Doug and his drinking. I felt a bit like a spy.

We were packed into the ballroom like sardines. The crowded room seemed to bounce to the beat of the music as the laughter and chatting reached a fever pitch. It was late, loud and my high heels were killing me. Through the haze of cigarette smoke I saw Doug across the room still sitting at the bar.

I walked over to tell him I wanted to leave. Only when he opened his mouth to speak did I realize he was, as he would say, "hammered." He was slurring his words, completely intoxicated. I managed to navigate the way to the exit and throw on our coats. I supported him by hooking one arm through his, like an usher would escort a lady down the aisle. I fished out the car keys with my free hand as we stepped out into the cold winter air, a saving grace that snapped him out of his stupor for the five-minute walk to the car. He slipped into the passenger seat and I shut the car door.

*Designated driver again*, I thought, *no surprise there*. I drove home in silence as he quickly passed out, slumped over in his seat. I was pissed.

Arriving home, I parked in our pitched driveway. He woke and struggled to get out of his seatbelt. I walked toward the house, watching his struggle continue. Finally, he won the battle over the restraint and managed to stagger around the car and across the sidewalk onto the lawn. His drunken stumbling ended in a face-plant in the front yard snow. I entered the house.

"Where's Doug?" asked my sister-in-law.

"He's in the front yard."

She ran to the living room picture window. There he was for all to see face down in the snow. She cried out to my brother Patrick to rescue him.

"Leave him there," I said. "He's shitfaced again."

Patrick, who's like Switzerland, usually level headed and neutral, retrieved my drunken husband from the freezing temperatures. I left Doug to sleep it off on the couch. I thanked my brother and his wife while apologizing for the embarrassing drama. I checked on the children and felt compelled to sleep in their room on the floor.

That night was a turning point. Every cell in my body knew the marriage was over.

In the light of day, Doug and I began a heart-wrenching discussion about the future of our marriage and children. The love and trust we built were severely damaged. My head told me try to make our marriage work for the sake of the children, try to move forward as a family. He agreed to stop drinking, go to marriage counseling and Alcoholics Anonymous meetings. In that moment, he appeared to be genuine. Together we attended one counseling session and he attended one AA meeting. Two weeks later, he came home totally inebriated.

*That's it. I'm done.* "You've chosen the bottle over your family, I'll file for divorce," I said.

The energy in the house completely shifted. In an instant, we morphed into separation mode. Staking out territory in our small two-bedroom Cape, he slept upstairs in the newly converted attic, now a master bedroom suite, and I bunked downstairs with the kids. He worked rotating shifts, two weeks of days, two weeks 4 p.m. to midnight, and midnight to 8 a.m. every six months. He also moonlighted at one of the outlet stores. I used to grumble about him being gone so often, now it was a blessing. A meeting with my lawyer revealed I could not legally leave New Jersey with the children without Doug's consent. The new daily routine was put into play.

Doug continued to provide; he brought home the paycheck and, in his mind, that was enough. He had little to no interaction with the kids. My job was to take care of the children, the house and the dog. For the next year and a half, I camped out in the kids' bedroom. Each day I would wait for Doug to go upstairs to bed. Only when "the coast was clear" did I venture out of our room. It was easier to avoid any confrontation, to just stay out of his way and keep the peace. This daily event was always changing, dependent on his work shift. It was an intense situation and getting progressively worse. Now I knew what that hamster in the wheel felt like. I couldn't get out either.

The law forced me to stay put, but that didn't stop me from planning. I'd temporarily move in with my parents, enroll the kids in school and find employment as a teacher. My work schedule would coincide with the kid's school day and we would have snow days and vacation time together. I had my bachelor's degree and only needed one course to obtain my teaching certificate. I promptly enrolled in a graduate course offered in the fall of 1995 at my alma mater.

My neighbor, Alesia, who now had three young ones of her own under the age of five, was willing to watch my kids once a week for the semester. I don't know what I would've done without her help. Week after week I attended evening class, picking up my sleeping kids in their feety pajamas at 10 p.m. and dragging the three of us home. Day after day attending to the children's needs, trying to do homework, housework and make the grade, I kept my eye on the prize: financial freedom. Some days I would plant the kids in the playpen with sippy cups and Cheerios for an all-day cartoon marathon. Some days I never got out of my PJs, but my course work got done and that teaching certificate was within reach.

WHEN DOUG WORKED the four to twelve shift, he started coming home late, two and sometimes three a.m., sometimes drunk, and sometimes he didn't come home at all. The gap between us was getting wide and deep. I always heard him when he arrived home; many times, I would pretend I was sleeping. The stress and fear of not knowing what was coming through the door each night grew into a routine of tense, sleepless nights. I began to grind my teeth so severely my jaw was aching by morning like I had been punched in the face.

One night, Doug came home under the influence again. The kids were asleep, and I was just coming out of the bathroom. He started making sarcastic remarks. I was sleep-deprived with frayed nerves, barely keeping it together on the surface. He started throwing his weight around. I had no filter; I made a snide remark back which quickly escalated into a heated argument. There we were breathing fire at each other. He got physically pushy; I attempted to grab his shirt, but grabbed the bolo tie around his neck instead and pulled him so close we were nose to nose. Spit was flying out of our mouths, yelling at each other in a fit of rage. I must have been out of my exhausted mind.

The next thing I knew, I was hurled across the living room. I landed on the floor face down. I didn't move. I was stunned.

He continued to rant.

I lay quiet, hoping to disappear into the floor, praying he would go away.

My prayers were answered; he blew right by me and dragged himself upstairs.

Slowly and quietly I picked my body up off the floor. I felt something wet on my back and I wiped it with my hand. I was bleeding. My back must have been punctured by a piece of metal on the old steamer trunk I used as a coffee table. I cleaned the cut and slipped back into the bedroom where the kids were surprisingly still asleep. I locked the door and lay down to digest what had just happened.

Like prize fighters, we took to our opposite corners of the house. I began to live on extreme heightened alert. I listened intensely to the sounds in and outside of the house; a car pulling into the driveway, a car door slam. I knew every sound and where it came from, every creak in the floor, every door opened, every door closed, the turn of a doorknob, all memorized and filed away. I swear I could probably hear the frequency of a dog whistle.

I locked myself and the kids in our room every night to keep us safe. One night I heard him coming down the hallway, stumbling around outside our bedroom door. The doorknob started to rattle. I remained quiet and pretended to be asleep and prayed he would go upstairs. After a few minutes the rattling stopped and he staggered back down the hall in what was most likely a drunken stupor.

*Thank God the door was locked.* I exhaled in relief and laid down waiting for sleep to overtake me.

# THE BLOODY WALL

The uncertainty of the night shift schedule was quickly instilling a visceral fear in my gut. Around 1:00 a.m. I heard a car door shut, peeked out the window and saw Doug staggering up the walkway, beyond drunk. The front door rattled. I had locked the screen door earlier that day so the kids couldn't open it. Something told me it wasn't safe to let him in.

I ran to the kitchen and locked that screen door and the wooden one behind it. I moved back into the hallway and listened. The screen door handle jiggled, then stopped.

*Thank God. He gave up.*

As I turned toward the bedroom, I heard a huge crash of breaking glass. I panicked, my shaking fingers struggled to dial 911. I could hear the echoing news sound bite of Nicole Simpson calling 911 when O.J. was breaking down her door. I told the dispatcher that Doug had just broken down the back door and that he was drunk, gave him my address and hung up. I ran back into the back bedroom with the kids and locked the door. The police arrived minutes later. They struggled with Doug in the kitchen.

Finally, an officer knocked on the bedroom door and told me it was safe to come out. Amazingly, the kids slept through this whole fiasco. As I gingerly stepped down the short hallway, I noticed blood smeared on the wall. Doug must have punched in the glass door with his bare hand. I knew he was trying to get to me.

Doug was sitting in our tiny kitchen with police officers surrounding him, hands cuffed behind his back. I caught a glimpse of his expression. His brain was clearly swimming in alcohol; he was seething.

Officers called a sergeant to the scene because Doug was a brother in blue, a detective sergeant in a neighboring town. They wanted to make sure one of their own was handled properly. They confiscated all his firearms from under the bed, in the nightstand and the hallway closet. I don't know if Doug was wearing his ankle holster that night. At least seven officers were in my house.

The sergeant asked if I wanted to press charges. I was sobbing. My head was spinning. *If I press charges, he could lose his job, lose his license to carry a weapon. We'd lose our house. How would we survive without child support?*

"No, I don't want to press charges," I said. The sergeant asked again, deliberately and slowly this time, an attempt to sway my decision. *He's probably seen too much domestic violence in his day.*

"No," I repeated. "Just keep him out of here overnight, let him sleep it off."

As I turned to walk into the living room, I saw Marianne scooped up in the arms of one of the officers. She must have wandered out of the bedroom while I was talking to the sergeant. I signed off on the form stating that I would not press charges. I thanked them all and locked the doors behind them. With the force of all my 110 pounds, I pushed the heavy oak kitchen table up against the side door.

I went back into the bedroom to tuck Marianne in and she looked at me with a big smile. "The cops, they love me, Mommy".

She was somehow unaware of the terror I felt that night.

I sat in the kitchen still in shock, when the phone rang. One of the officers Doug worked with explained he had picked up Doug and wanted to assure me he would keep him overnight to sleep it off. He added that Doug was so inebriated he took a swipe at him, trying to punch him out at police headquarters.

I knew Doug wouldn't remember much of what happened, if anything. I, on the other hand, remembered it all. Still, I couldn't leave the state without his consent. Divorce papers were being drawn up, but still were not signed; I was forced to wait. Somehow, we continued living under the same roof.

Doug's drinking habits were growing increasingly worse. He never drank hard liquor all the years I knew him, only wine or beer. Now he kept a bottle of vodka in the refrigerator. He began seeing someone he worked with at one of his moonlighting jobs. I secretly thought maybe it was a good thing. *She can keep him out of my hair.*

A HUGE SNOWSTORM WAS FORECAST, the cupboards were bare, and I needed to run to the local market for supplies. Doug was in the midst of his daily routine, preparing for his 4-12 p.m. shift. Every day like clockwork he would wake up, drink a few cups of coffee, go out for a run and lift weights in the basement. He had two pairs of running shoes that he would rotate to wear evenly, both clearly marked with numbers one and two. All this in spite of being a smoker. He took an extraordinary number of vitamins religiously, an attempt to balance out his unhealthy habits.

He argued with my request to watch the kids while I ran out to buy groceries before the impending storm. I stood firm and left abruptly, scrambling to beat the rush. An hour later, I arrived home with the goods; no offer from Doug to help lug in the bags. He was gone in a flash. Work seemed more important to him. We were left to fend for ourselves.

I cooked dinner, bathed the kids and tucked them into bed. The early evening darkness crept in and snowflakes reflected in the light of the street lamp. The blizzard would soon be upon us. I locked myself in the back bedroom with the kids and tried to sleep.

In the quiet of early morning I peered out the window to find Mother Nature had blanketed us in snow, with five-foot drifts blocking both house doors. Doug did not come home for the next three days, blaming it on impassable roads. For me it was a sorely needed respite; a blessing.

# THE DIAGNOSIS

*I*an had just turned three and wasn't talking yet. The pediatrician had said, "boys are slow," so I didn't pay much mind to it. I watched as the doctor used a Japanese pellet drum, a small drum attached to the end of a handle with beads tied to threads on both sides. He twirled it so the beads would strike the drum, making a rhythmic sound by Ian's ear while his head was turned. Ian did not respond. He never turned his head toward the sound. The doctor suggested that I schedule an appointment with a neurologist, just to be on the safe side.

*At worst, perhaps he's deaf, I could handle that. We would simply learn sign language.* The appointment was scheduled.

THE DAY ARRIVED and we entered the office, announced our presence and waited our turn. When called, I scooped up my three-year-old, walked through the door and down the hallway. As I entered the doctor's office I noticed a corner filled with toys. Ian happily started bulldozing his way through them.

I placed myself in the empty chair before the doctor, who intermittently observed my son while asking me a laundry list of questions, all impersonal, invasive, like an interrogation. Our consultation was over in about twenty minutes.

"Your son has autism," she said without a trace of bedside manner.

This was a foreign word to me. The next thing I knew I was escorted out of her office with an 800 phone number and the name of a book for parents raising children with autism. What was this thing called autism? What did it mean?

I tried to squeeze in a few questions before leaving. The response was "I don't know if you are in denial, but your child has autism." I was shown the door. I scooped up Ian once again, headed toward the parking lot, secured him in his car seat and then slipped behind the wheel. A wave of fear shot through me. I knew this strange and unknown thing called autism wasn't good news. My eyes filled with tears as I drove home. When we arrived, Doug was involved with his daily routine preparing for his afternoon shift.

"So, what'd the doctor say?" he asked pouring his coffee.

"It's autism," I said. "She told me he would probably never speak, feed himself, dress himself…"

"What? No, that can't be right," he argued.

My tears began again. "Well, that's what she told me. I'll have to get a second opinion." The residual shock still shivered up my spine.


OUR DIVORCE WOULD BE final in 1996, the year autism came into our lives, the year the kids and I would begin a new chapter. Doug and I had reached an amicable divorce agreement. We never really fought over anything aside from his drinking. We equally divided what had been accumulated over five years of marriage. In exchange for consent to leave the state with the children, I agreed to minimum child support.

We were headed to Cape Cod. I prepared all boxes to be moved and finally received my teaching certificate that spring. Everything was ready to launch. We just had to wait for a court date when the divorce would be final.

# MOVING DAY

It was early June and moving day finally arrived. Our belongings were packed, labeled and sprawled out on the front lawn. Doug and the kids were in the house. On this sunny, warm morning I sat on the front steps for the last time, waiting for my father and brother to arrive to help us move.

They arrived at 7 a.m. in my dad's pick-up truck towing a U-Haul. We exchanged "good mornings" and quickly got down to business. My dad assessed the size and shape of each item on the lawn and carefully selected each one for placement in the trailer. I shifted into supervisor mode, making sure anything fragile or of value was not harmed in the process.

We were in a whirlwind for about an hour. One by one the items disappeared from the front yard as my father and brother stuffed the trailer and truck to capacity. The task was complete. I glanced back at the house. Doug stood inside looking out the large picture window. It was surreal; a metaphor for how our marriage had failed. We were separate, emotionally and soon physically.

I entered the house to gather the kids and our dog, Sam. Sam would travel with grandpa in the truck. The kids and I would go in my tiny Tercel hatchback, the very same car I drove the day I was held at gunpoint, the day I met Doug. I buckled the kids in their car seats. My brother took the wheel. I slipped into the passenger seat, with the window rolled down.

Doug came outside and walked toward the car. He popped his head in the window saying his last goodbyes to the kids. He paused, looking at me, and said, "bye Jo".

I couldn't say a word. A flood of tears rolled down my face.

My brother looked at me and hesitated.

"Just go," I said, "just go."

He put the car in drive and we were off, without a plan.

*I'll figure it out when I get there.* I wiped away the tears and took a deep cleansing breath.

*Part Two*

# CHANGES

*"Circumstances does not make the man; they reveal him to himself."*
James Allen, As a Man Thinketh

# OVER THE BRIDGE

*F*inally on Cape Cod, over the bridge, the smell of low tide filled our nostrils as we headed east on Route 6, a one-way trip to start anew.

We had reached our destination.

At my parents' home, I unpacked only the essentials; the rest of my life remained in boxes neatly stacked underneath the basement stairs. We three would bunk together in the upstairs bedroom, picking up where we left off, but now without fear.

For the first three years after my son's autism diagnosis, I instinctively shifted into survival mode, determined to carry on even if just treading water. At age three, my son was too old for the state's early intervention services and too young to enter the local preschool program. He was lost in the rules of the system. Even with a diagnosis of severe autism, he didn't make the cut.

He was put on hold for the next six months, but early intervention was critical. I pursued numerous therapies on my own; traditional, alternative, even spiritual healers, almost anything noninvasive was worth investigating. Time and money disappeared like water running through my fingers. Meanwhile, patience was running on empty. I'm sure I had a nervous breakdown somewhere between 1996 and 1998, but I was just too busy to notice.

# ON MY KNEES

*I*n March 1997, the kids and I were still living in my parents' house. My parents were in Florida, keeping warm with fellow snowbirds, but would return with spring. I had spent the last nine months adjusting to cohabitating with my parents, being a single mom, battling with an alcoholic ex-husband and diving into a crash course on autism, including therapies, special education plans, medical support and the overwhelming costs that go hand-in-hand with all of it.

I am usually an optimist, a self-starter who finds "a way" through any quagmire, but one night it was different. It was 9 p.m., the kids had finally fallen asleep and the house was unusually quiet. I was cleaning up the dinner remains, wiping down the table and counters. Bits of food always dotted the floor beneath Ian's seat, followed by droppings leading through the kitchen and into the bath. Sweeping and wiping a new path, I restored order for tomorrow's breakfast rush. As I wiped up the last bit of crumbs, I found myself on my knees on the cold ceramic kitchen tile. Alone in the rare quiet, an exhale of exhaustion escaped my lungs. I was done.

Every muscle in my body seemed to receive the message: it was okay to relax. I felt like I'd been white-knuckling on the steering wheel, not able to feel the pain until I let go. An unexpected rush of heat shot through my body, blood pumping so fast I'm sure veins were bulging from my forehead. My heart was racing; I broke into a sweat and collapsed on the cold tile floor. Tears began to flow and my clenched fists pounded onto the tile.

"Why, God, why have you done this to me and my children? What have I done to deserve this?"

The floodgates had opened. I could barely catch my breath between sobs. For the first time since filing for divorce, I allowed myself to feel the sadness, the anger, the grief. For the first time in my life, I was angry with God. I had lost faith.

In that moment, the last shred of hope seemed to disappear. I lay on the floor like Raggedy Ann, drained and numb. I had been functioning in high gear for over a year and was now on call 24 hours a day, 7 days a week for a four and six-year-old who desperately needed their mother. I tried to balance my attention between them, but this is not possible for a single parent up against autism. Autism always wins.

Trying to keep the plates spinning in the air left me at a mere 98 pounds, operating on little sleep, 365 days a year, with no vacation, no pay. I lay on the floor blaming God for striking down my son, my family, with this thing called autism. *Had I not made all decisions in the best interest of the children?* It clearly wasn't enough. My life was out of my hands. Like a puppet on a string I continued, only to be further pushed down the rabbit hole of autism.

Ian, two and a half years old.

# AUTISM 101

*"Start by doing what's necessary; then do what's possible; and*
*suddenly you are doing the impossible."*
*- Saint Francis of Assisi*

Over the next seven years, I would conduct a one-woman campaign in search of support for my son. Like the old television show *Dialing for Dollars*, I was cold-calling and networking, collecting leads by word of mouth, hoping one would be a winner. No jackpot, but my efforts did pay off with a revolving door of therapists and educators. My son was now receiving weekly occupational and speech therapy provided through the Visiting Nurses Association. I secured funding through a nonprofit to pay for a personal care attendant to cover a few hours each week of respite. The elementary school contracted with a local nonprofit specializing in autism; its therapists taught me how to communicate, how to be with my own son.

## The Teacher

EVERYBODY HAS A TEACHER. My teacher appeared out of nowhere, a lightning bolt out of the blue. Structured and rigid, demanding my attention every minute of the day, a rollercoaster ride into an unknown confusing world of silence. Emotions expressed through screaming and kicking, bolting and biting, climbing and jumping. All without fear. All without boundaries. All without a reason. I had to relearn how to speak, how to see, how to anticipate the next moment. Autism is my teacher.

I was not allowed to fail. There was always a lesson before me. My only escape was ignorance, choosing to ignore the existence of autism, although I found this impossible. It was like gum on my shoe, sticking to whatever it touched. Every time I tried to wipe it off, it clung to something else. It never went away. The lessons have been hard and true: unconditional love, acceptance, structure and persistence. These are the teachings of autism.

It tries the depths of my strength when my energy is beyond depleted. I've known both the joy of its smallest miracle and the horror of its ability to wear me down. It has kept me guessing at how to reach my child, held prisoner in the silent world ruled by autism. Lessons have been learned about restructuring time, the language of occupational and speech therapies, special needs education and its federal laws. I learned about the brain and how it responds to diet, vitamin support and alternative therapies. I learned about the endless attempts to attain just one goal and the costs that went hand-in-hand with it, financially, physically and emotionally.

I learned autism is not accepted by all, and that you cannot go everywhere and do everything. I learned inclusion is not always a good thing. I learned I could not console my child's outcries and screams, but only try to discern between a cry for help and a cry of pain. I am in demand and autism is in command, twenty-four hours a day, every day.

I learned to watch my child like a hawk and guard him with my life, to sleep with one eye open and to sense when he is sick. I keep track of his eating and bathroom habits and pray he will have a bowel movement on his own, so I don't have to tackle and struggle with him to insert an enema. I pray I don't forget to check the B.M. calendar or forget the last time I gave him medication.

I learned there were few people who could watch over my child. I learned to live with limited sleep, limited time, limited activities, limited life. No vacation, no sick days, no pay.

But in those rare miracle moments, when my child's eyes look directly into mine for a few seconds, I know that he is connected with me in my world. That is my reward. It is a school like no other; so you do what's necessary, with high expectations of what is possible.

## The PEC System

MORE THAN ONE neurologist told me Ian would probably never speak. Through the Integrated Special Needs Preschool Program he was introduced to the Picture Exchange Communication System. The PECS, as we've come to know them, are small-line graphic drawings of items and actions with the associated word underneath. One PEC we used daily was a picture of a juice box with the word "juice".

These icons were cut up in small laminated squares with Velcro stuck on the back. The goal was to have Ian select what he wanted and Velcro it to a premade sentence strip that began "I want..." This was tedious. Day after day, I struggled to get two kids dressed, fed and out the door each morning to meet the buses. Now I was being asked to present icons for food, clothing and activities as part of our daily routine. Every morning was like *Mission Impossible.*

Ian's preschool teacher told me that if I started using the PECs, Ian might have language someday, but if I didn't, he would never speak. That's all I needed to hear. The PEC system was incorporated into the morning routine.

Everywhere I went, Ian went, and I talked to him all the time. I presented the PECS through the daily routines of dressing, eating, showering, bedtime, showing him what it was, repeating the word, hand over hand prompting him to select the appropriate square and secure the Velcro onto a sentence strip stating what we were doing, or what he wanted. Most of the time, Ian didn't respond. When he did, he just chose a random icon. Time, repetition and patience were paramount.

One day in the middle of my repetitious questions to Ian, I had a moment of doubt. *What am I doing? I'm just talking to myself.* I felt defeated, overwhelmed with frustration and grief that I may never hear the sound of my child's voice. In the wee hours of the next morning I thought I heard a voice say "juice." *Am I dreaming? Did my ears deceive me?* "JUICE", an insistent, louder voice bellowed.

I was up in a flash, fumbling in the dark, flying down a flight of stairs, scrambling for a juice box out of the fridge. I ripped it open, stuck in the straw and ran back up the stairs. I grabbed the PEC for juice lying on top of the bureau and displayed it while he was drinking. "Juice," I repeated, "nice asking for juice." The teacher was right. My ears witnessed a miracle. His first word, "juice."


### The Sound of 'L'


IAN SAW the speech pathologist regularly through the Visiting Nurses Association. She told me that he probably will never say his Ls because forming that sound requires a controlled use of the tip of the tongue behind the front teeth. She quickly added, "Vs and Fs may be difficult for him, too."

I went to work. Every night at bedtime, we practiced. I sat on his bed face to face with him making exaggerated movements with my mouth and tongue so he could see and hear the letter at the same time. "LA, LA, LA, LA. Ian says LA, LA, LA." And I praised him each time, even if he didn't repeat it.

Mastering the 'L' sound would take years, but today, even though Ian can't have a conversation, he can repeat back to me "I love you." I'm not sure if it has meaning for him, but it was worth every minute we spent practicing, rising above yet another challenge.

### Ian Ties His Shoe

ANY OTHER DIVORCED parent with two kids could have found a job, an apartment, placed the kids in daycare or after-school programs and carried on. Autism changed everything. Just being employed was a major feat. My life revolved around after-school therapies, doctor appointments, and mandatory special needs education meetings. A resume of skills, experience and education doesn't matter; time is minimized by the demands of autism.

I apply anyway. I need the work and I want to work, even though it feels like swimming against the current. Like many wash-ashores on the Cape, I've held a laundry list of part-time jobs. I've worked as a medical clerk, office assistant, and receptionist. I've made natural oils and cream products in an herbal store and cleaned houses for some locals. All of this was a far cry from my North Jersey employment at a fortune 500 communications company, complete with business trips and expense account. That type of work was history now, left in the dust plowed over by autism.

I was lucky to secure part-time employment as a receptionist at a chiropractor's office in town. The job was good for me on many levels. I could make a little money, interact with people and feel like a useful adult. I got small doses of normal on a daily basis, just what the doctor ordered. Many times when I was at work, the school nurse called to say one of my kids was sick and needed to be sent home. A single parent always has a higher rate of absenteeism. The chiropractor was flexible and kind about my family situation.

One day, Ian's special needs teacher called. I panicked at the sound of her voice. "I wanted to speak to you personally," she said. After what seemed like a forever pause, she continued. "Ian tied his own shoe today."

I began to cry. I could hear the emotion in her voice as she admitted, "we were crying, too. We've been working on this for a long time now. Ian has been working very hard. Finally, he did it today. We'll continue to practice so he doesn't lose this skill. I am so proud of him."

In that moment, my heart was full of joy, an emotion that was almost extinct. This was a major achievement for Ian. I knew more possibilities awaited.

## Universal Language of Song

In 2006, Ian entered the regional middle school, comprised of sixth, seventh and eighth grade students. His special needs teacher was teaching him his name and phone number. It was right before vacation week and Ian would be out of school, out of structured routine and at home. He was entering adolescence so getting his full attention was not easy, I was now up against autism and hormones.

Ian loves a bath, a sensory treat that is very calming. I would always sing songs and give him water toys during bath time. I thought about the goal of teaching him his name and phone number and thought I'd give it a whirl. One night while he was in the tub, I sang his name and phone number to the tune of an old song I sang as a kid when we played jump rope in the street. "My name is Ian, this is my phone number, nine-O-eight three-four-four zero-one-seven-nine." I sang the song over and over every night at bath time that week. On the third day, I purposely dropped a few words. As I took a long pause, he filled in the blank. He was listening and downloading the song in his head all along.

By the end of vacation week, with verbal prompting, Ian was able to sing his name and phone number back to me. The vibration of song and repetition helped him process and retain the information. He was listening, following the rhythm. Communication through the vibration of music goes beyond words. Music, a universal language all its own.

## Communication Book

FROM THE TIME Ian entered preschool, a communication book was put into play, a notebook that traveled back and forth from home to school on a daily basis containing information about his needs and behaviors. Due to Ian's inability to understand and speak, this communication book was critical to his eating, medical, and bathroom needs.

**4-1-99, Morning entry from home**: *Meltdown this a.m. early. Don't know why. Pinching, crying (real tears). Wanted something but unsure what. I made him sit until he was quiet, then let him go. He got over it. Hope the rest of his day is better.*
Johanne

**Reply from teacher:** *Lots of a.m. aggressions today but settled down after lunch somewhat. Didn't touch his sandwich. I threw out the*

*cut-up half. Ian is superstar next week. Can you help us with a list of*
*favorites, i.e. favorite movie, favorite place, favorite food, etc.? Maybe*
*16? Try for at least 14.*

I would always cringe when I received a request like this. Ian's favorite things? It was the $64,000 question. How was I going to conjure up a list that long? I could count on less than ten fingers his favorite things to do and the food he liked to eat: swinging, jumping, music, cheese, pizza, ice cream, Cheerios, chicken fingers and bagels. At age six, this is what he lived for, lived on, this was it. No favorite toy or movie. No favorite color. Inclusion was a challenge for all of us.

**7-15-99, from the teacher:** *Really tough day today with Ian. Went swimming – he bolted seven times and then ripped off his bathing suit. I made him get out of the pool, put his bathing suit back on and then do work. He bolted a lot today and actually bit another child, something he hasn't done for a <u>long</u> time. He seemed just plain exhausted – needed a lot of hugs. Ended on a good note – got through all programs with no problems. Then he got to swing. Hope you have a great weekend. Glad to hear doctors went well. PS Eye contact excellent today.*

These reports made me sick to my stomach. I felt so sorry for the child he bit. I felt powerless, not knowing how to control Ian's behavior, not knowing how to help him. I feared they would ban him from swimming, an activity so important to his sensory diet. I wanted to respond by being level headed, emotionally detached. I stated my experience and observations along with suggestions of possible solutions:

*Sorry about the bite – hope it wasn't serious. He will do this, even to himself at times of extreme frustration. Having the bathing suit problem at home too – maybe a speedo would be less irritating to him. Lots of bolting out into the street here at home too. Seems to be pushing boundaries. Spontaneously requested an egg this weekend – a word not usually repeated. Had a good O.T. session Thursday afternoon and started therapeutic horseback riding on Friday. He did well there too! Hope today goes better.*

*Johanne*

**4-11-05, Morning entry from home**: *Ian was up several times last night – flailing, screaming – he used to keep me up many nights like that when he was little. No breakfast, may tire easily – seems more resistant to requests. Asked for what sounded like 'television' last night (We have had no TV temporarily so it wasn't even in the room!) Hope he calms down for the day.*

*Johanne*

That was one of many nights of lost sleep for both of us. At age 12, Ian was entering adolescence and losing sleep would quickly drop to the bottom of my concern list. Hormones and autism would prove to be a nightmare combination.

## Pouring Rain

IT WAS POURING RAIN, a Sunday, and we were locked inside for the day. My parents' T.V. room had organically mushroomed into the kids' play area, filled with toys, a therapy ball, overstuffed pillows of Pokeman characters and favorite movies. The room had four walls, a door, two windows that locked and no sharp-edged tables, a place where Ian would be stimulated while safe and corralled.

Ian was unpredictable. He would jump, bolt and climb at every opportunity. He didn't answer to his name. He had no safety awareness. I kept him under close watch always. We continued to sleep in the same room, with the door and windows locked every night. We spent most of our time in the playroom if we couldn't get outside. It was early evening, I turned my back for one minute, leaving the door ajar. When I popped my head back in to check on the kids, Ian was gone. Marianne hadn't noticed he left.

I flew through the house checking each room. I looked out the window. No Ian. Through the living room and up the stairs I went, where there were two bedrooms. I looked to my right, no Ian. I searched the room to my left, still no Ian. Then I noticed the window was wide open.

My heart was pumping on all cylinders. There he was, sitting on the roof of the farmers porch, his knees bent, quietly still in the dark in the pouring rain. He was a few feet from the window. I climbed out quickly, grabbed steady hold of him and carefully brought him back through the window, landing on the bedroom floor. I could barely catch my breath. Our soaked, shivering bodies held together for a few moments of relief. I held him so tight, I couldn't let go even though we were safe inside.

## Exhaustion and the Gym

I WAS CHATTING with the therapist after one of Ian's sessions when she paused and looked at me. "You look tired," she said. "You know you probably have borderline exhaustion, right?"

No, I didn't. It was like a lead balloon had landed on my head. She went on to tell me these kids take a lot out of you and to make sure I was taking care of myself. There I was, 98 lbs., size 2 and too busy to notice. I was almost a walking skeleton. It was a wakeup call I couldn't ignore. Mothers aren't allowed to be sick, it's a union rule. That week I dug out my Visa Card and joined the local gym. I honestly couldn't afford a gym membership, but my body was screaming *JOIN, you can't afford not to.* I needed to keep my immune system up and working; I needed to fill my empty well.

I returned to the gym the following week for my free introductory personal trainer evaluation. He took one look me and with fear in his eyes said, "you don't want to lose weight, do you?"

"No," I said, "the opposite. I want to build some muscle and gain weight." The tension left his face as he exhaled. "That's harder to do," he said, "but it can be done."

We set up a plan. Religiously, I would go to the gym four times a week; my parents watched the kids. I had to wait until they were asleep because Ian was so hard to handle when he was awake. The gym closed at 9 p.m. so timing was everything. Of course, nothing's perfect, the kids were sick at times or just had a cranky night and couldn't fall asleep on time, so I missed those nights. But on most nights, as tired as I was, I dragged myself to the gym and usually felt revitalized when I was done. It not only improved my physical health, but saved me mentally. Like a mini vacation it got me into a zone light years away from the ruthless demands of my existence.

## Being Present

LIVING within the restraints of autism kept me in financial ruin. It was like trying to keep a Band-Aid on a bleeding wound that really needed stitches. I couldn't work full time. Ian required care 24/7 and I could only find respite funding to support him ten hours a week, although I was grateful to have that. I was also grateful to have Katie, who loved my children as much as I did. She had been Ian's 1:1 Educational Assistant when he was in elementary school and knew him well. I could trust him in her hands without worry.

Autism was tearing away, shred by shred, at the core fabric of our family. I kept patching up the holes like I did with my favorite blue jeans in high school, making them wearable, but sometimes they were barely hanging from a thread.

*Just begin*, I would tell myself. *Don't worry about tomorrow. In this moment I am safe, my kids are safe.*

I came home with grocery bags that day and invited Katie to stay for dinner. "Today we eat!" I shouted. Yet another feast made possible by the assistance of food stamps.

In that moment the bleeding stopped, the holes were patched and the fabric of family stood strong.

## Milestones & Miracles

It was a typical Thursday afternoon; the kids were having their snack after school and we were waiting for Mr. B, the occupational therapist who provided Ian with weekly one-hour visits through the local Visiting Nurses Association. Mr. B had been working with him for about a year, so Ian was quite familiar with him. Fortunately, I was able to obtain a computer through an Easter Seals program that loaned computers to those with disabilities at no cost. It was a large, refurbished, computer with a separate CD tower most would consider a dinosaur, but to us it was golden. It opened a window of opportunity for Ian to learn language in a way that I could not otherwise afford; truly a gift.

Mr. B had been working with Ian on one-finger typing, hand over hand, copying the word that appeared on the PEC. He patiently showed Ian the PEC, repeated the letter, showed him the letter again and then typed each letter, hand over hand, one at a time. "Popcorn," Mr. B would say, "P – O – P – C – O – R – N," pausing and typing between each letter. "Popcorn," Mr. B repeated. When they were done he praised Ian. "Ian typed popcorn, good job!" He gave Ian a few pieces of popcorn. A reward always followed Ian's work.

The lessons always began with Mr. B presenting two items that Ian could choose to earn. When Ian became impatient, Mr. B would calmly remind him, "first work, then ..." the reward. Sometimes Ian chose a favorite snack. Sometimes he chose a video, trampoline or swing.

As Mr. B came through the door one afternoon, Ian took one look at him and began to cry and tantrum. Seeing Mr. B meant he was going to have to work and he clearly wanted no part of it that day. Very calmly, with a smile, Mr. B said, "Hi Ian." Ian kept up his tantrum and tried to open the slider to the backyard. I made sure it was locked, so he couldn't bolt into the yard. "First work, then swing," Mr. B said in a sing-song voice.

With that, Ian bolted out of the dining area, through the living room and up the stairs to the bedroom. I darted after him. When I reached the top of the stairs and caught my breath I entered the bedroom that now served as a therapy/computer room. Ian was sitting in front of the computer, hunting and pecking letters on the keyboard. Mr. B quietly appeared and we both moved closer to Ian, watching nothing short of a miracle unfold before us. Ian was typing the word SWING.

"Oh my God, he wants the swing," I said in a quiet voice. *It's in there. He understands.* Mr. B and I looked at each other in disbelief, amazement and joy. We had just witnessed what for us was a miracle, born of persistence, trying to get beyond the silence of autism. Ian had reached another milestone and had certainly earned his swing.

## More Miracles

IT WAS POURING rain so fast and furious I couldn't see past the hood of my car. Highway traffic slowed to a crawl, walls of water appeared in the blink of an eye from travelers going too fast in the opposite direction. Cars were pulling off to the side of the road, but slowly and carefully I kept going, moving forward. My sister and I with three kids between us, ages six through eleven, were all packed into my small Tercel hatchback, headed for an evening mass; a special healing mass about 30 miles from home. As I pulled into the church parking lot, the rain transformed into a light mist while the last light of day faded into darkness. There were so many cars, I was lucky to find a parking spot.

One by one we piled out of the car. Ian was still small enough for me to pick up; I carried him through the darkness into the church. The place was packed, like a rock concert, but this rock star was a priest, a healer. Marianne went with my sister and her daughter to squeeze into a pew inside; I hung back with Ian in the foyer.

The crowd, the noise, the unfamiliar surroundings were all potential triggers that could put Ian into sensory overload. I needed to be in a space that he could tolerate. There was a "Cry Room" for the little ones and I could see parents and their toddlers through the glass walls. *No, that wouldn't work. If a baby began to fuss or cry it might trigger a meltdown for Ian.* I found a chair and remained in the corner of the foyer with Ian securely seated on my lap.

There we sat as people trickled in, blessing themselves with holy water. Some were milling about, chatting and finding their seats, awaiting the well-known healing priest, Father D. A couple of local parish priests ran back and forth in the foyer, no doubt tending to last-minute details before this renowned healer took to the podium. It was difficult to keep Ian busy and in place for any length of time. He was overactive and made noises that I was used to, but startled others. He always needed to be moving or stimming, shaking a string, squishing a ball or eating reinforcing treats.

Several priests gathered in a group at the far side of the foyer, like a football team in a huddle, discussing the game plan. The group split. As we sat waiting, Ian began squirming and making noises. I tried to keep him calm by stroking and rocking him gently. One of the priests came straight toward us. I thought for sure we were going to be asked to leave.

The priest who stood before us was Father D. He smiled and laid his hands on Ian's head, quietly said a few words that I did not understand, made the sign of the cross over him, turned and left without a word. He had just given Ian a healing blessing.

In the midst of Father D's busy preparation for Mass, out of the many in the chaos of this needy crowd, this man was drawn to Ian. Divine intervention had blessed my son, a healing without words.

## Invisible

THE WET, warm liquid dripped down my hand. I was bleeding. Ian had a grip on me like a dog on a bone. His eyes were on fire, teeth gritted as he swiped the side of my face, like a raccoon swipes at food. An adrenaline rush sent me into auto-mode, appearing outwardly calm. "Quiet hands," I demanded. Ignoring the behavior, I continued to check out my groceries. My fourteen-year-old autistic son was having a meltdown in the supermarket. I managed to write a check, thank the cashier and direct my son to push the cart toward the doors.

Just beyond the exit doors, he caught me off guard and pushed the cart full force across the parking lot; thank God there were no cars or people in its path. His meltdown was gaining force. It was just getting dark. Fear was vibrating every nerve in my body. I could barely see my car only a few feet away in the shadows of dusk. If I could just get him in the car, we'd both be safe.

I continued to lead him closer to the vehicle. He thrashed out at me again. This time his attempt to strike was blocked by my one free hand while the other held onto him for dear life. I managed to fish keys out of my purse, opened the door and maneuvered Ian into the backseat. "Sit," I demanded. Adrenaline flowed through my veins in full force. "You are all done," I said in a firm, low voice reinforcing my verbal prompt with sign language.

I got behind the wheel and my head slumped down into my chest. I broke down into a flood of tears. Ian and I were in a cold, dark parking lot. My five-foot-five, 125-pound teenage son was assaulting me and no one stopped to help.

*What if he had bolted into the dark? I would never find him. What if he had seriously injured me? Who would find me in the dark? What if?*

When you love someone with autism, you hold on as tight as you can, even if he is beating you up. His life depends on it. I wiped the tears from my face and took a deep breath. Ian appeared calmer now. I started the car, turned on "The Chipmunks" music and continued home, as if nothing had happened. Passersby just kept walking, like we didn't exist. We were invisible.

## Courage

"IN THE FACE OF ADVERSITY, God asks you to do the right thing," said the man who stood in front of me. I couldn't tell his age. He was shabbily dressed in jeans and a sweatshirt. His teeth were grayed and salt-and-pepper stubble grew from his face. He was about forty, fifty perhaps? We stood in a church. A long line extended into the all-purpose room where government food was being distributed. *How did I get here?*

It was surreal. I became the observer. The never-ending line was a patchwork of humanity—young, old, fat, thin. Some people were dressed neatly, some in worn and tattered clothes. Some were dirty, some were clean. I found myself judging those around me, when in fact perhaps I was judging myself.

Inside the room, four elderly female volunteers were seated at two long tables. The woman at the first table was checking IDs. "Sign in please," she said. As I added my name to the list, the old woman continued, "Do you have a Mass. Health card?" Anyone poor enough to qualify for Mass. Health insurance also qualifies for government food. I dug into my purse and fished out my wallet. Producing the card confirmed that I was officially on or below the poverty line. Like the get-out-of-jail-free card in Monopoly, it allowed me to move to the next station.

Moving on, I was assigned a volunteer to take me around the makeshift market of folding tables stacked with cans, jars and boxes. Behind each table was yet another volunteer to replenish the goods and assist with my selections. I couldn't imagine such personal service at the local market. With free government food I was treated like royalty.

The tables were arranged in a horseshoe, each displaying items such as cereal, vegetables, and powdered milk. As I approached each section, the voice behind the table asked, "How many in your family?" My reply determined the number of items I could take. The smiling faces of the volunteers genuinely conveyed their kindness, friendliness and even respect. Even so, it was quite difficult for me to maintain a shred of dignity.

I felt exposed, naked. I kept swallowing, swallowing hard. The lump in my throat seemed to expand into a tennis ball. I thought that if I just kept swallowing maybe I could hold back the tsunami of tears. *Why was this so hard for me?* I had been through so much more and survived. *Was the universe punishing me for making bad choices?*

It wasn't enough that I was divorced with two kids. It wasn't enough that my son had severe autism. It wasn't enough that I couldn't work and support my family. It wasn't enough.

I realized that I wasn't done surviving. I had yet one more lesson to learn, humility. I took a deep breath to regroup. My energy shifted. I reminded myself that my children are my reason to get up in the morning, my reason to continue. So, I swallowed and moved forward to humbly receive the next can of peas and jar of peanut butter.

Autism bled into daily life, affecting our family financially, physically and emotionally. In 2006, I found myself under pressure so great it brought my ability to work to a grinding halt. Every ounce of my energy, every minute of the day was spent meeting the ongoing demands of autism and the daily follow-through of programs that carried over into the home. It was exhausting. Every day felt like I was performing solo on a high-wire without a safety net, not knowing where my next step would take me.

# REINVENTING THE WHEEL

*D*espite my challenges with divorce and autism, I never lost the vision of having a home of my own. I kept looking at real estate brochures, touring houses on the market and chatting it up about what my home would be like. I wasn't even employed at one point, but I never gave up. I applied to Habitat for Humanity and other affordable housing projects in 2000. Nothing surfaced, but I kept the vision of one day having my family in a real home, our home. A couple years later another Habitat home was planned in the town where I worked part-time; I applied again. In 2002, on a cold night in February, the phone rang. The voice coming through the wire was telling me my name had been literally picked from a hat of three family names; all who qualified for Habitat homes. I was in shock. I tried to register what had just happened. *Was this for real?*

I pushed the buttons on my landline. "Dad, are you sitting down?" I said.

"What's going on?" he asked.

I took a deep breath as the words slowly spilled out. "You're not going to believe this, but I was chosen for a Habitat for Humanity home".

"What?" he exclaimed. "That's unbelievable!" I told him about the build, about the hours of sweat equity required. Habitat requires all home-owners to participate in the building, even if they've never swung a hammer! Friends and family can help out too.

"I can help build," my dad said. "We're coming home."

I had gone through a thorough application process, followed by an intensive interview about my family and why I needed this home. I can't remember what I said, but I was passionate about providing a family life for my kids. For me, finding a home was never a question of *if*, but rather a question of *when*.

A couple of days later, I was in the dining area of my parents' house with my daughter when a strange car pulled into the driveway. Two people walked toward the house, one carrying balloons, the other flowers. Two representatives from Habitat for Humanity were welcoming me and my family into their housing program. I felt like one of Ed McMahon's Clearing House winners! I accepted their gifts and formal confirmation that my family had been selected for the new home to be built in Orleans.

From the moment we landed on the Cape my daughter would often ask "Mom, why are we doing this?" referring to any uphill battle I was trying to conquer in that moment.

My standard reply, "I'm reinventing the wheel."

I closed the door behind our visitors trying to digest all that had happened. When I turned around, there stood my daughter looking back at me. "Mom, you finally did it, you reinvented the wheel."

I smiled. "I did, didn't I?"

She had been listening all along.

# REINVENTING THE WHEEL PART II

*T*he dedication of our new home would take place on October 30, 2002, the night before Halloween, the night the Celts believed the veils were the thinnest between the worlds of the living and the dead; a belief that the spirits would provide guidance in predicting the future. Being second generation of Irish descent in America, the magical placement of this day was no coincidence; it was meaningful synchronicity.

The final touches were being put on the house and I was told that I was expected to say a few words at the dedication. Volunteers and community members would gather on site. A local pastor would offer a blessing, the director of the local chapter of Habitat for Humanity would speak and then it would be my turn to take center stage. I have a deep fear of public speaking. I hate it. I stepped into the center of this circle of kind-hearted people, with my blood pressure rising. My heart began to pound so hard I thought for sure someone would hear it.

I knew I couldn't just "say a few words" off the top of my head, so I wrote something down the week before. The paper I held in my hands was shaking. I tried to remember to breathe and prayed my voice wouldn't crack. Then I heard myself:

" 'It is when you give of yourself that you truly give.' A quote from the book The Prophet, by Kahil Gibran. How do you say 'Thank You' to so many for so much; friends, family, even strangers who gave of themselves, their time and their talents to contribute to my family's well-being? How do you describe the heartfelt gratitude of being given the opportunity to make a life, a life of our own, to be a family? How do you thank so many, for being a living example for my young daughter that amidst the darkness of war in the world there are many who still give from their hearts and that miracles really do happen? You cannot imagine the impact you have on other people's lives. With every nail, every shingle, you are not only building a home, you are building pride and dignity for the family who will live there. There are no words to describe how grateful I am for this blessing, so I will simply say Thank You. Thank you very, very, much."

My children and I were being supported by the universe. The hands of many came together to ensure our family's future.

Heart-shaped knot on the porch post, a reminder that our Habitat house was built with love, 2002.

# ACCEPTANCE

*It is well to give when asked, but it is better to give unasked,*
*through understanding.*
*- Kahlil Gibran*

*A* gift card fell out of the envelope. Through eyes blurred with tears, I realized there were *two*, both from my local market. Our Christmas of 2006 was like no other.

My life had crumbled around me once again; another attempt to rebuild our family disappeared. My new husband had announced that he was leaving the marriage, without explanation, without delay. Left with two children to feed, bills to pay, no job and no child support, I was in shock. He had adopted my children as his very own only eight months before; what was he thinking? Had he gone mad? How would we survive?

I scrambled to get food stamps and stood in line for government food. There was no room for pride. After two months, child support was finally enforced, but with that came attorneys' fees and more bills. I felt like I was drowning in legal documents and overdue statements. I was frantic, constantly moving, thinking, doing, keeping all the dishes spinning in the air, afraid to stop, afraid one might fall and break, afraid that I might break. I couldn't afford to even think about it. I just kept moving.

Our divorce was final by summer. That autumn, I learned through legal documents that my ex-husband had remarried immediately after our divorce. He had moved on to a new wife, a new life, and left us in the dust. I was no longer in shock, but still digging out from the wreckage he had left behind, and Christmas was upon us. How was I going to conjure up a holiday for my children when we were barely making it through each day? One afternoon Mr. B arrived for his usual OT session with Ian. We saw him so often he had not only become a good friend, but was lovingly considered extended family. He very kindly said, "you are in need," and insisted he would ask his church to select my family to donate to this year. He explained that the church not only provided gifts, but also a holiday turkey dinner with all the trimmings. I was overwhelmed by the kindness of this heartfelt gesture.

Instantaneously, I struggled with pangs of guilt, the ultimate acknowledgment that we were, in fact, a truly needy family. If we were to receive this gift, had I failed as a provider for my children? We could certainly use the food. I was always trying to get to the next step, through the next day, the next week. I thought of the children. Once more, there was no room for pride. I accepted his offer with gratitude. He asked what toys the children might like, what their sizes were and what they needed.

I managed to get a tree that year and buy a few small gifts. The week before Christmas Mr. B came to drop off the gifts and turkey dinner. He arrived carrying a large box brimming with food, including a homemade pie ready to bake in the oven. He returned to his car to gather up the finely wrapped bags and boxes, all tied in ribbons and bows. It was all so humbling. I reached out to him with a grateful hug. After he left, I stood with my children among the bundles. We were surrounded by an abundance of gifts, food, and love for community, for humanity, for each other.

We were in fact a family in need, a family stranded in circumstance, limited by choices impacted by autism. Mr. B had rallied community members, complete strangers, who were all willing to give of themselves without condition to help a human being in need.

Another life lesson of acceptance.

# AUTISM & ADOLESCENCE

### Track Marks

*I* was on the phone with the director of special needs of the local public school district. She was asking invasive questions about Ian, about his behavior and could I handle him. In a nutshell, she was asking "Was I safe?"

She wasn't alluding to something I didn't already know, but she triggered my emotions. My acting skills automatically kicked in, my voice business-like while the tears of suppressed fear silently streamed down my face.

When I hung up the phone, the floodgates opened. I had survived that conversation, one more battle, but the war was not over. I stood in my kitchen looking down at my arms, at the numerous scars and scabs, some of the wounds still black-and-blue, the color of eggplant, remnants of the aggressions I endured during my son's meltdowns.

I was scheduled to attend an IEP meeting the following week. It was June and the weather was already hot. No matter, I would have to wear my long-sleeved shirt. I felt like a heroin addict covering up tracks. I could not let them see the wounds; it would just give them more reason to push me in a direction I wasn't ready for. I needed more time to think about Ian's future. I sucked it up, put on my long-sleeved shirt and pretended not to sweat.

## Residential School

MY FRIEND KATIE took the wheel that day. My brain was imbalanced, my nerves frayed. I was beginning the most difficult journey of my life. The drive would take about two hours, the destination a residential special- needs school where I would leave my 15-year-old autistic son and begin yet another chapter in our lives. The heart-wrenching decision was made. The time had come to place him.

My journal entry that night read:

*March 2008*

*The day finally arrived; there was no turning back. It was surreal, but oh so familiar. I remember when he was four years old and I went to look at a school that offered an alternative therapeutic approach to autism. I found myself observing two boys, only five and six years old themselves, through a one-way mirror. They were walking across elevated boards, about two feet from the floor, that had holes like Swiss cheese. The boys slowly maneuvered to the end of the board with the assistance of the therapist. It ended at the top of a slide where they slid down into a small ball pit. The interaction between the boys and the therapists was disjointed. I was overwhelmed, thinking, could this be my son?*

*Today, eleven years later, once again I look through a one-way mirror. My son on the floor in a circle with his new classmates, smiling and laughing at the other children playing duck-duck-goose. He seemed happy; I cried. I walked away feeling like I was just kicked in my chest. I had to go. I had to trust he was in good hands with these strangers. He has a new home now, a new school, new friends and moving onto a life I could never give him.*

*You don't have a choice with autism, you must always decide what is in your child's best interest, not your own. Each decision feels like a walk through fire, learning to let go and realizing even liberation can be bittersweet.*

What I failed to write in my journal that night was the visceral effect this experience had on me. As I stood watching Ian through the one-way mirror at his new school, my knees literally buckled, blood drained from my head and I almost fainted. I grabbed onto Katie's arm and she kept me from falling. She supported me as we slowly walked back to the car and I slipped into the passenger seat.

It was a surreal day and a quiet night. The trajectory of our lives was changing, driven by a force larger than ourselves.

# TRANSITION

*T*rudging through an emotional swamp, I felt I had finally reached the other side. My son had successfully transitioned into his new residential school and we had all survived. I rested on what I perceived as a plateau, licking my wounds. Just when I thought I could breathe, the universe delivered yet another autism experience, one that would repeat itself indefinitely.

"I still cry every time he goes back," said the mother before me. Her seventeen-year-old son diagnosed with autism had been living at a residential school for the past seven years.

I felt confused. What she said didn't make sense. *Hasn't she gotten used to the visiting routine by now? After all, seven years, that's a lot of coming and going. Perhaps she's too emotional or too attached.*

Fast forward. Now it's my turn. I survived the heart-wrenching decision to place my own son in a residential school at the age of fifteen. I survived the eight-month search for the right school. I survived the heartbreaking "goodbye" on the day I left him there, knowing he couldn't come home for thirty days. I survived handing over my vulnerable child to complete strangers, trusting, because I had no choice. I survived the feeling that I might not be able to live through it or live with it. But I did, and I am, so why should she cry after seven years? Surely it should be routine by now?

My son came home for his first visit from his new school, excited and happy. It was wonderful to be near him, and yet it was strange at first. Even though he can't speak, I could tell by the look in his eyes that he felt it too. It took a few minutes to adjust and mesh our energies back into family mode. To my surprise, I cried, uncontrollable tears of joy, relief, and suppressed grief. And I understood that I, too, will probably cry for the next seven years. In that moment, I understood being emotional is not weak. We don't have to "suck it up" or "get over it." We need to feel it to make way for new energy, new possibilities, and maybe even healing.

## Transition Part II

IT HAD BEEN several months since Ian had been placed at his new residential school. I would find myself still waking in the middle of the night, wandering into his room to check if he had kicked off his blankets. He wasn't there. The bed was neatly made and the room empty. Alone, I stood in the dark absorbing the reality check. Slowly, I found my way back to bed with a heavy heart and lay down, trying to disappear into my pillows. Life had changed once again. I loved him enough to let him go. It was in his best interest. It was inevitable.

Another autism lesson, a different kind of heartbreak. It took Ian two months to adjust to his new surroundings; it would take me the next two years.

# GRIEVING

*I* don't remember the day I announced to the world my son had been diagnosed with autism. The declaration must have emerged on its own. I'd never even heard the word before Ian's diagnosis in '96. With that one word, the war had begun.

Neurologists, psychologists, occupational therapists, speech therapists, and educators lined up to assess my child, all with the same endpoint; autism. Each day a challenge, each one a small step toward a goal that most children achieve through incidental learning, by watching others. The baby I gave birth to, the new life that I had cradled in my arms, that I believed was a healthy baby boy, was about to rock our world with a different story. Life would never be the same.

In his toddler years, I noticed eye contact was not quite right. No words were spoken by age two, but the pediatrician assured me "boys are slow." By age three I had almost convinced myself he was deaf. Autism was about to bloom. Nonstop craziness was about to explode into our lives.

But what about the child I gave birth to, brought home from the hospital with hopes and dreams of a future filled with possibilities, what about that boy? What about little league and fishing with Grandpa? What about his first kiss and graduation day? It was all gone, sucked out by one word, autism.

It felt like the time I fell five feet from a tree fort when I was a kid and got the wind knocked out of me. Panicked, I ran into the house gasping for air. My mother put smelling salts up my nose, jolting me back into a normal breathing rhythm. The diagnosis knocked the wind out of me. I couldn't breathe. But my boy was gone forever, taken prisoner into the silent world of autism.

The onslaught of assessments and doctor appointments that followed leaked into the ears of family and friends. They talked around the diagnosis, not knowing quite what to say, acting like it didn't exist. No one really wants to talk about it, so they don't; it's the "white elephant in the room." Our society wants us to always look on the bright side and suck it up. Certainly no one acknowledges the child you thought you gave birth to, the grief you feel at the loss of your healthy newborn.

When someone dies, people surround you with emotional support. They bring food, spend time, talk to you about your loss and listen. I would put my life on the line for my son like most mothers, but I lost a child to autism. No smelling salts can fix this one. A deep void was left in my heart, no one to listen, no one to validate the loss. I suffered alone in silence learning the only way to heal was to feel my way through it. No one lets you grieve.

**Cry of the Lone Wolf**

ANOTHER MOTHER RECENTLY ASKED, "Does the feeling ever go away? Do you find it has given you strength?" She was referring to my decision to place my severely autistic son in a residential school.

She had placed her daughter, now twenty, who is much higher functioning neurologically and living with bipolar disorder. Now a legal adult, she lives on her own, but unfortunately doesn't take her medication and refuses counseling. She's not spoken to her mother in three years because of the placement.

"Does it give you strength?" I repeated. "No, but you have to be strong to survive it."

We paused a few moments, then I continued, "Does the feeling ever go away?"

We both knew what she meant: that deep sadness, that "howling cry of the lone wolf," the feeling of indescribable despair. "I don't know if it goes away," I said. We hugged. Acknowledging it was a way to process, to move forward somehow.

It brought to mind a lesson my daughter taught me back in early spring of 2002. Nine eleven was fresh in our minds. We were all wounded in our hearts and souls. And our dog was dying. We knew his days were numbered.

Our Keeshond was my daughter's best friend. Now he laid on quilts in the basement being hand-fed and bathed several times a day. My daughter brought all her stuffed animals, dogs of course, downstairs and surrounded her dying friend with "family." She sat herself in a small chair, read to him, talked to him, nurtured him, comforted him the best she knew how.

The final day arrived. I dreaded the thought of breaking the news. That evening, I quietly told her of his demise before her nightly bath. She was inconsolable. She cried and cried as the shower washed over her and blended with her tears. She talked to her departed friend, loud and angry. He had left her. The sadness in her voice, so deep, sounded like the heartbreak howling of the lone wolf. I could only be there for her, listen to her, hold her. Mommy could not make this better. This was a life lesson of her own.

Perhaps it's something you learn to live with. You shift your perspective. You let go. If you keep a tight hold on it, it's like wearing a tourniquet. The blood will stop. If you loosen up, it will flow.

When we let go, we invite possibilities into our lives, even if it's just getting to the next step. We need to honor the process, honor ourselves.

## Empty Nest

I WAS SHOVELING a January snow off the walk on the front side of my house. As I finished clearing the last heap of the fluffy frozen coating, I noticed a bird nest tucked into my bare rose bush. Frosted in a layer of snow, it sat perfectly formed in the middle of the twisted twigs of thorns that remained; an empty nest from last spring. I grabbed my phone and captured the image. It was a perfect metaphor for how we try to raise our kids under our protective guard only to give in to the inevitable hourglass of time. What once nurtured life is now empty; the baby birds have flown and a new season has begun.

It was a glaring reminder of what most of my generation, the Baby Boomers, were experiencing; an empty nest. The kids have moved onto college, marriage or their first apartment. Change is afoot and the path of uncertainty begins.

Empty nests for parents of special needs adult children like mine are a bit different. Although we share the void, the vacant bedroom and the resounding silence, our adult children have not moved on; for them it's a changing of the guard. Their caregiving needs change hands. Their new home is a group home with housemates like themselves and caregivers who meet their needs 24/7; this is their new extended family.

When our children turn 18, parents like me are required by law to shift into the new role of legal guardian, where we continue to manage our adult children's support programs and affairs through

88

nonprofit organizations and government agencies. Like most parents, our nests become empty and the inevitable reality of growing up moves our children forward into adulthood, but our responsibilities as guardians remain for a lifetime. The nests are empty, but ours echo back the deafening question, *"Who will step into my shoes and watch over my child when I am gone?"*

Although my son has moved out of the nest, he will never fly solo. For me, empty nest is not just a moment of transition; it's another leg of the journey into the uncertainty of caring for him beyond my lifetime.

## Rogers Law

ACCORDING to the Guide to Rogers Guardianship, "A guardian for an adult is a person appointed by a judge in the Probate and Family Court who is given responsibility to make decisions for an individual after a judge has decided s/he is not competent to make their own informed decisions." It further explains, "At a Rogers Guardianship hearing, the Court is asked to authorize extraordinary medical treatment for an Incapacitated Person." The guide goes on to state that this usually refers to treatment with antipsychotic medication.

THE TIME HAD COME; Ian turned 18 and was emancipated by law. I was about to take on the role of Rogers Guardianship. I retained a lawyer to guide me through the necessary legal documents. The list included a Rogers Review Order for prescribed medication, a Treatment Plan, a Clinician Affidavit, a Care Plan and a Supplemental Report, all signed and submitted for the judge to review and approve. Rogers Law monitors medication dosage and, put bluntly, protects the disabled individual from being placed in a chemical straitjacket. Each year this formal legal review is conducted. The psychiatrist, nurse, behaviorist, social worker and the team caring for Ian, as well as myself, provide the data. A court-appointed lawyer visits Ian and submits his own report. Emancipation launched Ian and me into a prelude to adult services for the disabled.

There I sat chatting with my lawyer about the proceedings, in a courtroom waiting for the judge's approval of Ian's first Rogers Review. The court-appointed attorney representing my son came across the room to introduce himself. He had met and observed Ian at his residential school earlier that month. In a friendly gesture, he offered to shake my hand. It was a moment of truth; one more reality check. I returned the handshake and smiled. As he returned to his seat on the other side of the courtroom, I lost the fight to suppress my emotions.

Silent tears streamed down my face. The heartbreak was so intense I thought I would melt into the wooden bench. I was about to be stripped of my right to motherhood. I walked through the doors of the courtroom that day as a veteran mom and left no longer recognized as the mother. In the eyes of the court, I am now legal guardian.

*Part Three*

# CHOICES

*Fall seven times, stand up eight.*
**Japanese Proverb**

# TURNING 22

## Adult Services

*T*he public school career of special needs students like Ian extends beyond the average graduation age of eighteen and ends on their twenty-second birthday. Turning twenty-two signals a transition time into the world of adult services. Special needs day programs replace the school day and group homes replace their residence supported with round the clock staff. Both are federally funded by the Department of Developmental Services (DDS).

This transition is not automatic. All must apply, qualify and be approved for funding. Even if a student has been provided special needs services in the public school for nearly twenty years, you must still qualify.

Once approved, a search, application and acceptance of placement into a group home and day program follows. Timing, availability and funding are all critical to the process. Without proper planning, applicants could end up on a very long wait list.

# Happy Birthday

AGE 22 IS the magic birthday for all those diagnosed with autism severe enough to require lifelong supports. All the services provided since Ian's diagnosis just got downgraded, literally overnight, due to his turning 22. Happy birthday. The trajectory of his future hits a wall. The safety net is gone. We are now navigating choppy waters looking for a life preserver, but it just doesn't exist. I was led to believe a transition plan would ensure a continuum of care; the reality is quite different. I rose to the occasion and secured housing and care at an exceptional group home for my son, feeling lucky. For most, options for housing are slim to none. The waiting list could take years.

## The Process Begins

**AUGUST 2014**

As legal guardian, I picked up the phone and initiated Ian's transition into Adult Services. Based on the search I experienced in 2008, trying to locate a residential school that actually had an opening for my son, I wanted to allow plenty of time. I agreed to have the first meeting with the DDS local office in my home.

On a hot August afternoon, two female representatives arrived at my door, the Adult Service Coordinator and her supervisor. It was a friendly meeting; intake forms were filled out with general information about Ian's needs. The entire meeting took about an hour and ended with the exchange of handshakes and smiles; it triggered a flashback. I recognized those fake exchanges; they were the same back in the day at corporate meetings and events; these women appeared to be wearing the same social masks. I played along and paid attention. When I inquired about searching for a placement for Ian, they assured me I had plenty of time, not to worry, they would be in touch.

*Okay,* I thought, *they know the drill. This is what they do. I'll wait to see what unfolds.*

## September 2014

It seemed that every time I turned around it was Monday and before I knew it, September had creeped in. I had not heard from DDS and wanted to get the ball rolling. One night while looking at Ian's residential school website, I noticed the words *Adult Services* in a small text box and I clicked on the link. His residential school was expanding and offering Adult Services group homes. I immediately clicked on the contact info and sent off an email to the Program Director. Within days I was able to secure a place for Ian in one of the group homes; a synchronistic blessing. We had a history with the organization, a well-established positive relationship with staff, familiar faces and people who understood him. The staff, medical and administrative support had been consistently positive over the past seven years and I knew this was the best place for him. I sighed in relief, knowing I was halfway to the finish line, but not knowing that last leg would feel like the Boston Marathon, running up Heartbreak Hill.

## October 2014

Fall had arrived and the DDS Service Coordinator now informed me her office was not familiar with day habilitation programs outside the Cape and the Islands. What does *that* mean? She knew last month I had secured a group home placement for Ian off Cape, why is she telling me this now? Do they have no idea what exists outside their territory? This did not compute.

The Official DDS Guide Book for Transition Planning stated it was the office's role to assist with identifying and securing supports for individuals like Ian. I had already done half the job by locating a group home and all they can do is report they are not familiar with day habs off Cape? I had no time for debating this point. My son's future was at stake.

Being unfamiliar with the process, I sought guidance from a familiar contact, Ian's future group home director. Margaret was a wealth of information. She suggested two day habs located not far from Ian's future group home. She contacted both and immediately had dates scheduled for me to tour the facilities. I visited both. One appeared to be a good fit for Ian's needs. It was clean, well-staffed and clients were engaged in activities.

On October 17th, I receive an email from the Adult Services Coordinator, Terry. She informed me that *we* needed to choose a day habilitation program and to keep her informed. It was clear to me she wasn't doing her job, I was; there was no *we* in this search. I had no more time to waste waiting for Terry to step up to the plate. Stumbling through my own inquiries, I found out it was part of the mandated procedure that I complete an application and request that DDS send a referral packet to this day hab. When the paperwork was complete, the day hab director and behavioral clinician would observe and assess Ian. I completed the application and requested the packet be sent. All boxes were checked and all steps were taken. Almost a month later, on 11/19, DDS finally mailed out the referral paperwork.

As we approached Thanksgiving, I was feeling more hopeful that things would be settled before the New Year, before the end of March deadline, Ian's 22nd birthday. There was a lull in email exchange and I trusted the process of reviewing his application was in motion. Three weeks later I received an email from Terry. Attached was a copy of an email sent to her from the day hab program director. The day hab had no openings. There was a waiting list and it was not known if an opening would be available in March to accommodate Ian.

My heart sank. Why was I not told this back in October? Why would I tour a facility that did not have openings? Why waste time observing Ian and processing paperwork? Why did Terry not research this? I had just wasted three months on a facility that knowingly was at capacity and had no place for my son. Now what? I turned once again to Margaret for direction and clarification. I forwarded the email and asked, "What happens if there's no opening come March?"

She assured me there were plenty of other day habs in the area and that she had given Terry the name of the DDS Service Coordinator outside the Cape Cod area who can make recommendations. I promptly sent an email to Terry. *"It is a priority Ian be in a program that is safe, providing well trained staff who understand his needs. The director of the day hab did not state how long the wait might be. I will contact her about the number of people on the list. Let me know if other programs might be an appropriate fit for Ian. Thank you."*

Again, a long pause followed. I was hoping this time Terry was busy searching for potential day habs. On December 29th, I received an email from Terry asking what kind of assistance Ian would require. Was she kidding? She's supposed to be coordinating the foundation of my son's future. She's asking for information that was provided during the intake nearly five months ago. If she had bothered to look in his file, the same information was provided on the original application to DDS that qualified him to receive services in the first place. Now she wants it again? Who hired this person?

I took a breath, mumbled "one more time" and immediately replied: *Ian requires 24/7 supervision especially when out in the community. He needs bathroom supervision as well as supervision during eating and all other activities. His needs are detailed in his*

*Individual Education Plan (IEP). I can resend if you need another copy.*

January 2015 rang in with a roar followed by a winter that pummeled New England with relentless blizzards. Three-foot drifts blocked my doorways. Boston had record snowfall, 45.5 inches in the month of January alone. No way could I get over the bridge to visit day hab facilities on the mainland. Mother Nature decided I needed to sit tight, research, regroup and take a breath; Happy New Year.

February brought more of the same; ice and snow. I was literally frozen in place. Phone and email became my lifeline, the only tools I had to keep the conversation alive while my son's future hung in the balance.

On February 6, I received an email from the day hab where Ian was on a wait list, the first one I visited. *"Still at capacity with no foreseeable openings."* I quickly reached out to Margaret, who recommended two other programs and offered her program supervisor to accompany me on a tour. Mike knew Ian fairly well. Finally, someone who would know what program would best fit Ian's needs.

On February 17, Terry emailed to say it's *crunch time.* If there wasn't a day hab opening for Ian, he would come home and live with me until there was one. Is she kidding? I've been doing all the work, with little to no assistance from DDS, and she's telling me it's crunch time? Seven months into this search, this woman has no idea who Ian is and what his needs are.

My fingers took over the keyboard: *No way can Ian come home during the interim. This would become a safety issue. I am unable to care for him as a single parent. I know others ran into this situation and an extension was made at the school to allow time for placement. I am stuck in the snow and ice and unable to visit any programs this week.*

Later that day, I was compelled to clarify: *I find this situation extremely disturbing. I inquired about day habs late last summer and was told I had time. I tried to begin this process last fall. Most of my assistance has come from Ian's future group home staff. This potential for Ian to not have a place to go upon his 22nd birthday seems to be the result of lack of planning. Compromising his and my safety is unacceptable. Please forward the name and number of someone I can discuss this with if you are unable to help.*

Terry's reply was, not surprisingly, less than helpful. Instead of providing an alternate solution, she informed me that extending the stay at residential schools was no longer possible, that regulations had changed. She went on to say these transitions increase anxiety for everyone. And ended with an odd comment acknowledging she *heard* from me that it would be unsafe to have Ian home. What does that mean? Was this a weak attempt to make me look like a Nervous Nelly about the transition process and shift blame? We were in crunch time, as she put it, because of her lack of participation in the search and planning.

*Enough,* I thought, *I am done dealing with her incompetence, time to go above her head to the Area Director, her boss, Darold:*

*I am forwarding this string of emails so you know the background. This is a dire situation that requires immediate attention and resolution.*

He promptly replied, acknowledged that this was a problem and he would do everything to resolve it. He went on to say that Terry felt I was focused on only one day hab program, the first one I visited, and said it was crucial I apply to other day programs immediately, and that Terry would assist. He said he was committed to finding an appropriate day hab placement for Ian by his 22$^{nd}$ birthday and ended with the old *don't hesitate to call me.* Something wasn't right, this was an email of mixed messages.

Darold said he was committed to finding a placement and yet instead of telling me *how* he was going to remedy the situation he put it back in my lap. If he's so committed to this search, then why am I the only one searching? I was floundering my way through the system, one Google at a time, searching for options with no assistance from his office. No, I would not phone him. Every conversation from here on out needs to be documented. The emails took flight.

*Darold, Thank you for getting back to me so quickly. I have just finished completing another application and am sending it via email to Terry to expedite tomorrow. The reasons the first day hab program was my choice were 1) it was an intensive program and 2) I was only given the names of two day habs to visit. DDS did not provide other programs to investigate. I sought guidance from the residential school staff where my son is currently placed and they provided two more recommendations I researched online this morning. These recommendations are the two applications that are in process now. If I had not reached out to the staff, I would not know about these two. This process should have taken place last year when I originally addressed it with your office. The lack of guidance and planning will jeopardize our safety. I am an aging single parent and my son is literally head and shoulders taller than I am. I, too, hope we are able to place him in an appropriate program by the end of March. In the meantime, we need a "Plan B" in case they are all at full capacity. Please advise how we might handle this going forward. Thank you.*

Darold's reply admitted something should have been done last year and assured me Ian would be placed by his 22$^{nd}$ birthday. His office would provide updates and devise a Plan B. At this point, the words and actions of DDS caused me to take great pause; I had lost faith in its integrity and the role it was supposed to play in this process.

My son's future was in the hands of a local agency that had no real interest in his well-being. He was one of many getting lost in the shuffle of the system. Someone in authority needed to know what was happening down here in the trenches, but who?

# THE LETTER

$\mathcal{I}$ sat at my kitchen table and wrote a letter to President Barack Obama.

*March 1, 2015*
   *Dear Mr. President,*
   *I need your help. I am a single mother of two young adult children. My son has severe autism. Over the years, I have struggled to keep a balanced home environment and am blessed to be a proud owner of a Habitat for Humanity home. In 2008 I had to make the heart-wrenching decision to place my 15-year-old son in a special needs residential school. However, for the first time since his diagnosis, I was able to seek full time employment. For the past seven years I have been working as a special needs education assistant in the public school system. Inspired by my experience with my own severely autistic son, I felt compelled to give back to the community by helping other children. The accumulated knowledge and skills, both*

*personal and professional, have enabled me to be effective in all classroom settings, severe, moderate and learning disabled.*

*My son turns 22 in March 2015. He will be forced out of the public school system into the world of Adult Services. I have experienced little to no support from the Department of Developmental Services (DDS) during this past year, an important transitional year. The task of searching for an appropriate placement in adult day habilitation has been placed on me. Although it is the job of DDS to provide guidance through this transition, I found myself scrambling to locate and network day habs in the area where he will live in a group home. Now in the 11^{th} hour, I am running into the challenge of no openings. Day Hab programs are at full capacity. My son requires an intensive program. When I asked DDS what could be done for my son while we continue the search for an appropriate placement, I was told he would have to come home. I cannot believe this would even be allowed. The reason he was approved for an outplacement in a special needs residential school at age 15 speaks volumes.*

*I am a single parent. I will be 60 years old in June 2015. My son is literally head and shoulders above me. Requiring him to move back home would be disastrous, jeopardize his safety, my safety and displace me from the workplace. I would have no means of support and would lose everything I've worked for including my home. My son should not have to suffer as a result of DDS's lack of planning.*

*I am asking for your help in changing the way DDS handles these transitions. People like my son are not just a number; they have lives and families, too. We need more day habilitation programs and housing to accommodate these young adults. 1 in 68 are diagnosed with autism. An estimated 500,000 will turn 22 and transition out of public and residential schools nationwide over the next 15 years. We are not prepared to receive this deluge of young adults with autism. Where will they go? This could surely overwhelm the healthcare system.*

*Being more than aware of the need, I am trying to be part of the solution on a small scale. For the last four years I have held the position of secretary on the board of directors for a nonprofit building housing for adults with autism. I was one of the original handful of parents who launched this grass roots movement in 2011, to create meaningful and dignified lives for adults with autism. This year we closed on a parcel of land. We are actively fundraising and raising awareness of the increasing need for a community like this. This model would not only provide housing but also structure, support and integration in the wider community.*

*Autism is beyond epidemic proportions. Although diagnosis and early intervention has improved, there is still no cure. Yet, no one is planning for the imminent tsunami of aging young adults with autism. I ask that you make this a priority of national conversation in healthcare. Education and awareness are key to the solution.*

*Thank you for listening. Respectfully,*

I STAMPED and sealed the envelope with a wish and a prayer someone would read it. I mailed it on March 1, 2015.

A few days later, I told a friend about the letter. She strongly urged me to send another one to Senator Elizabeth Warren. Why didn't I think of that? When Senator Warren was campaigning locally on Cape Cod back in 2011, I heard her speak at a coffee shop in town. At that gathering, I met Senator Warren's personal assistant and told her about the grass roots nonprofit I was part of and our vision to build housing for adults with autism. She graciously gave me her business card and said to let her know if they could be of any help. Four years later, I still had that business card in my wallet and it was time to act on the offer. I emailed, attaching the letter I sent to President Obama.

To my amazement, I received a reply email at the end of April and was introduced via e-greet to Senator Warren's legislative aide who is specifically assigned to Autism Policy. This aide was willing to speak with me personally on the phone! She gave me a half hour of her time, listened to my story and then told me what Senator Warren's office was working on regarding autism. I was blown away!

## The Search Continues

THE TIME-CONSUMING PAPER trail began again; back to protocol square one. Two more day hab applications were completed and referral packets mailed. Visits were scheduled for March 4th. Terry, Mike and I would tour the facilities under the guise they both had openings.

Aimwell Alliance day hab was sandwiched between local businesses in an old small strip mall. The receptionist greeted us and explained that a Zumba class had just finished. She acknowledged that the program director was expecting us and we were quickly escorted into another room. Pieces of the floor boards were broken, some missing; the building was clearly old and run down. We entered a conference room where we were joined by the program director and two staff members. The director explained the current program and showed us the floorplan of a new facility being built at another location to be completed by fall. Most of our visit was spent behind closed doors in that conference room discussing Ian's needs.

Finally, we toured of the rest of the building where staff and clients were. It took all of fifteen minutes. I saw no female clients, only men; not young adult men, older men sitting at tables in an open kitchen area. We were led down a hallway and shown a large empty room that had a lot of windows and dirt on the floor. Our tour guide said it was the greenhouse, although there was not one plant in sight. Other small rooms with closed doors we were not shown. The staff seemed guarded and not friendly. This place clearly was not for Ian. It was dark and unfriendly, with much older clients. No one was engaged in activity, and the building was literally falling down. I couldn't wait to get out of there.

Terry, Mike and I thanked the director for her time and headed to the next potential placement.

Glenwood Center was a delight. It was in a large brick building set way back from the main road. The receptionist buzzed us in, welcomed us with a smile and introduced us to our tour guide. The building was spacious with plenty of windows. We toured a sensory room, workout room, a cooking room, table top activity room, a leisure area with couches and a cafeteria. Staff and clients appeared happy and friendly as they went about their morning activities, not hesitant to acknowledge our presence. The program was explained as we walked through the facility and our questions answered. We weren't confined to a conference room, instead allowed to walk around to experience, observe and get a feel for the program. This was a relief. This could be Ian's placement.

The IEP official transition meeting marking Ian's move into the world of Special Needs Adult Services would take place at his current residential school on March 10. Since 2008, Ian's IEP was under the jurisdiction of the local public school located on Cape Cod even though his residential school provided the program. Over the past seven years the local school representative regularly attended Ian's IEP meetings. Jean was always a wealth of information and support. This meeting would be her last.

We crowded around the conference room table, Ian's residential school staff, including the nurse and social worker, Margaret, Terry, Jean and me. Ian's IEP and his needs were discussed. Now the big question, where does he transition to? The Glenwood Center program was still up in the air, no guarantee he would be placed there, no guarantee they had an opening. Terry, the Adult Services Coordinator, had no new programs to explore and there was still no Plan B as promised by her boss Darold back on February 17th.

As we approached the big question, Terry nonchalantly, almost with a sense of arrogance (or maybe ignorance) suggested I may want to revisit the Aimwell Alliance program; it had openings. *Of course it has openings, no one wants to go there!* I had already sent Terry an email clearly stating I would not even consider this program, so why would she make that suggestion at this meeting? I politely told her that program was not a good fit for Ian. She went on to quote my earlier email saying "Ian can't come home." I agreed that was true, however, Aimwell Alliance was still not a consideration.

As everyone sat listening, witnessing this ridiculous suggestion, Terry went on to challenge me three times with the same quote and three times I replied this was not a consideration. *Was I speaking another language? What was it she didn't understand about the word no?*

The room became uncomfortably quiet. No one else at the table said a word. We had hit the wall. The meeting was at a standstill. There was a white elephant in the room with a neon sign hanging from its neck flashing *DDS Has No Plan for Ian* and no one wanted to say it out loud. So, I put the ball back into play and asked the question, "Are there any other day habs in the area to consider?"

The social worker suggested we look at a local program, Windingway Place. She knew of other former students doing well there. She volunteered to call, to see if we could tour the program today, and promptly stepped out to her office. Minutes later she returned with hopeful news. We could tour the facility right after our meeting and it had an opening. It happened to be ten minutes from our meeting place. Without hesitation, Jean and I jumped in the car.

Windingway Place was located in a congested part of town, in a brick building abutted by other brick buildings housing various businesses. It had multiple levels and was filled with clients, some engaged in activity, some not. It was clean, with a ratio of seven clients to one attendant. That seemed rather high to me, but I quickly learned this was an accepted average ratio commonly found in adult day hab programs. I walked away with mixed feelings. It wasn't the best program, but it wasn't the worst, like Aimwell Alliance.

I went home with the assignment to complete yet another application and request a referral packet be sent to Windingway Place. Time was slipping away and Ian needed a safe place to go. Despite the confrontation initiated by Terry during the transition meeting, I went home that afternoon, tapped into my corporate social skills and sent her an email:

> *Thank you for coming to Ian's transition meeting and touring Windingway Place. I've decided the best fit for Ian's needs would be the Glenwood Center program. Please let me know the status of that referral. Thanks*

Terry's reply assured me we should have a decision from Glenwood Center soon and she would follow up. The following day Terry left a phone message saying we should not close any doors, followed by an email that stated the same, alluding to the idea of reconsidering Aimwell Alliance.

Once again, I needed to clarify, reiterate, send smoke signals, somehow make her understand that I was not interested in Aimwell Alliance. I was tired of being polite; my son's future was hanging by a thread. No more Mr. Nice Guy! My clarification email took on a life of its own:

> *I am informing you again, take Aimwell Alliance off the table, it is not a consideration for my son. I wish to move forward with Glenwood Center. If need be, I will seek legal counsel.*

In response, Terry left me a phone message that included *don't threaten me*. What she failed to realize is seeking legal counsel was not a threat; I was informing her of my next step. If she persisted, I would protect my son's rights. It was time to start moving up the food chain. I emailed Darold on March 16, 2015:

> *The search for a day hab placement for Ian continues. Considering his 22nd birthday is less than two weeks away, I would like to request he be maintained at his residential school until an appropriate placement is secured. His residential school has already accepted him into an adult group home. Please advise, thank you.*

Darold's response later that day once again assured me his office was making sure all was covered.

ON MARCH 17, 2015, an email comes out of the blue from Terry. She had contacted the off-Cape DDS office and got the list of day habs in the area. She actually called three of them; two I had already contacted myself back in the fall. She also contacted another facility, Community Corners, that I had already been exploring. Terry actually told the staff that based on other program assessments of Ian, he would need 1:1 support staff; which she said did not seem to faze them. *Wow, Terry had finally made an attempt to help me.* As they say, she was "a day late and a dollar short." Too bad she hadn't done this in 2014. We were now in the 11th hour and unless she could pull a rabbit out of that hat, we're screwed.

That same morning, I received an email from Mike that appeared to be bending toward the ear of DDS. He said he understood how stressful this process could be and that even though the choices on the table were not *first choices,* structure and support for Ian needed to be put into place and that I should reconsider.

*Was I not repeatedly advocating for Ian's needs; what was he talking about?*

The email went on to say individuals are not always accepted into the programs parents hope for. He knew of other individuals like Ian who transitioned into both Aimwell Alliance and Windingway Place and were doing well. Something wasn't right. I knew Mike's organization depended on DDS funding to survive. *Was he was being politically correct, walking a fine line to stay in the good graces of DDS?* He was probably told, *"You should not bite the hand that feeds you"* by his supervisors. However, Thomas Szasz questions the proverb and warns: "But maybe you should if it prevents you from feeding yourself."

I was feeling uneasy, unsupported and alone. Each step needed to be accounted for. I was becoming *The Documenter*. I felt an immediate need to protect myself, to document what was unfolding. The adrenaline was flowing. Something told me it was important to recap, clarify and chronicle the chain of events that had occurred with DDS. The uneasy feeling about mixed messages from DDS was now spreading out like an infection into Mike's organization and I wanted to make sure he and others were aware of what actually had occurred. I replied:

*I told DDS that I am not interested in Aimwell Alliance. Although the program and the new building layout sounds wonderful, what actually occurs on a day-to-day basis appeared to be quite different. I agreed with your remarks after the visit; the staff seemed very guarded.*

*As far as Glenwood Center is concerned, I believe it supports 1:1 clients. If staffing is the issue, perhaps this could be funded by DDS. Regarding Windingway Place, I received the application yesterday and will complete and return this afternoon. During my tour, I was not able to observe the second floor where I believe Ian would be (I saw one of his former housemates there). However, I was*

*given the firstfloor tour, which is soon to expand. I observed little to
no engagement/activity with clients, which is a concern.*

*Even if a placement were made today, transportation appears to
be an issue at both locations. Terry's suggestion of hiring a monitor
and placing Ian in a taxi with two strangers is clearly a safety
issue. Also, the anxiety about transition is really going to be around
Ian. He will be anxious and act out. My job is to make sure decisions
are made in his best interest, always, not based on dates. I began this
process with DDS in August 2014 and it has provided little to no
information regarding day habs. I handled the group home
placement and secured funding through DDS and Social Security;
those supports have been in place since 2014. Now, in the 11th hour,
DDS sends a list today of potential day habs, which should have been
provided six months ago. Most of my guidance has come through Ian's
residential school for which I am grateful, however, we've lost a lot of
time. I have contacted DDS in regard to a Plan B should we need
one. Please feel free to contact me by phone as well.*

I felt like I was about to be ambushed. The feeling triggered a
flashback to ten years earlier when I was under attack in a child
custody battle with my children's birthfather, Doug. I could not
afford a lawyer and opted to legally represent myself in New Jersey
Superior Court. I prepared an entire notebook documenting unpaid
medical bills and child support, as well as evidence of him almost
never exercising his visitation rights. I detailed both of my kids'
needs and how they were being cared for. I made two sets of note-
books, one for me, one for the judge and sent it by overnight
express mail. The same documentation before the judge was before
me as I sat at my kitchen table and made a court appearance via
conference call. My preparation, courage and conviction paid off; I
won. It was time again to roll up my sleeves and go to work. The
next day, March 18, 2015, I fired off another email, this time to
Darold: *"I have not heard back from you and am wondering about the*

status of a Plan B regarding my son's placement. *Since we are only a week away from his 22nd birthday, what happens if there is no day hab placement available to him? Please advise. Thank you.*"

That same day, his reply said he was out sick and would get back to me once he was back to work, that I should not worry, that we'll figure something out even if it's only temporary.

*Temporary, what did that mean?*

# WE HAVE A PROBLEM

On March 23, late afternoon, Darold emailed to say Windingway Place day hab would not accept Ian. He said they *would not* accept, not *did not* accept; this spoke volumes about Ian's needs. Darold acknowledged we now had a problem. Day hab placement needs to happen first, otherwise Ian would not be allowed to move into his new group home. He said he had been optimistic that Ian would be accepted, but it turned out otherwise. Darold clearly did not know Ian's needs and still had no Plan B. He said the alternative was for me to reconsider other options and closed with *please advise how to proceed.*

Honestly, I expected more professionalism and support from the Area Director; instead I received more of the same I had experienced with Terry. He was just hiding behind another title, placing the onus on me.

I felt like Astronaut John Swigert must have felt during the Apollo 13 Mission when he said "Hey, we've got a problem here." Like the Apollo 13 crew, I was stranded in unfamiliar territory, once again back where I started eight months ago. Where do I go from here? Even though Apollo 13 ultimately had to abort its mission, the men were rescued. Time after time my plans were aborted, too. Application after application brought the same replies, no acceptance, no openings, Ian requires 1:1 staffing, unable to support. All I knew was Ian had to be placed in three days and failure was not an option.

## Placement

I was later copied on the email from Windingway Place day hab detailing why Ian was not accepted. *Ian needs a program specializing in autism services that offers a rich sensory diet and peer environment that supports his needs*; Windingway Place's program was not able to accommodate him in this way. Darold neglected to say that Ian was rejected due to his high needs. That was telling; his intention was quickly being revealed. The momentum was picking up and emails began a back-and-forth rhythm like a ping pong game.

It was March 23rd, three days before Ian turned 22. My email to Darold read:

> *How do we proceed from here? Forcing Ian to come home jeopardizes his safety and as a single parent forces me out of the workforce without income. Glenwood Center had an opening but did not accept Ian due to lack of staffing to accommodate my son's high needs. Could DDS provide funding to hire appropriate staff? We need an emergency plan A.S.A.P. to move him into the available group home and provide day supports until a day hab program is secured. Please advise.*

Darold's reply stated we could consider funding staffing at Glenwood Center, but stressed that I needed to be flexible finding a short-term placement while pursuing my first choice.

*Why was he still focusing on this first choice thing?* There is no first choice, I'm pursuing anything available that will support Ian's needs.

Darold went on to note that Ian moving back home was not the plan and then said Ian would only go home if DDS couldn't find a placement that was acceptable to me. *What? He contradicted himself.* Clearly, he's trying to cover his tracks with a fabricated paper trail. Darold's Plan B was to force Ian into any program that would take him; that left Aimwell Alliance, never my choice, never in the running.

## Legal Counsel

As I embarked on the transition into Adult Services back in August 2014, someone suggested I might need a disability lawyer to help in the process. I took the name and number and filed it. Now I was faced with a life changing situation for my son that was unsafe, a decision based on a deadline instead of in his best interest. A decision not made by his legal guardian, but by the local DDS office, which saw him as a number, another dollar sign in the budget. I had no choice but to seek legal counsel; I dug into my reference file and pulled out the number.

I brought the lawyer up to date on the events that had occurred during the past seven months. She promptly sent a letter to the local DDS office one day prior to Ian's 22nd birthday. It indicated that this was in fact a situation that forced Ian to be placed under crisis conditions and declared this move to Aimwell Alliance be recognized as a temporary placement.

Her words appeared to fall on deaf ears. DDS continued to drag its feet without concern for the consequences to disabled individuals and their families. DDS seemed to be waiting me out, trying to wear me down. I needed to protect my child, his safety and well-being.

Ian's birthday happened to fall on a Thursday that year. His new group home was run by the same organization that oversaw his residential school, so he had visited his new home several times with familiar staff. Ian was moved without an issue that weekend into his new surroundings. Attending the dreadful Aimwell Alliance Program would soon follow. I was filled with despair imagining him in that awful place, alone and scared; it made me sick.

The universe decided to provide a pregnant pause and for the next several weeks Ian remained at his new residence with 1:1 staff while the Aimwell Alliance Program scrambled to get the required paperwork in order, transferred, and signed by me all prior to his entrance. I was secretly happy about the delay. It bought me more time to search for new programs, to try to find one that would support him, one that would accept him, one that actually had an opening. This pause allowed me a moment to breathe, to think about how to move this disastrous situation forward. Time was of the essence; my son's safety was now in jeopardy.

## The Letter Part II

IT WAS a late June afternoon in 2015; I had just picked up my 24-year-old daughter from work and was heading home. I reached the top of my driveway, put the car in park, and hopped out to check my mailbox. I grabbed a handful of envelopes and slid back into the car. Glancing at this pile of mail I noticed the return address on one white business envelope, it read: The White House. *Why would The White House send me junk mail?* In the few seconds it took to reach the bottom of my driveway, I realized this might be a reply to the letter I sent back in March. Stunned by this possibility, I turned to my daughter. "This might be a reply to my letter to President Obama."

"Open it!" she demanded. I carefully unfolded the letter. It was on White House stationery with a raised seal and what appeared to be the president's personal signature written with a felt-tip pen. As I read the words aloud, tears rolled down my cheeks. My brain was trying to process what I was hearing myself say. We both sat in the car stunned by what we were experiencing. My letter had been selected out of the tens of thousands received by the White House every day. My letter was chosen to be read and answered personally by the President of the United States. President Obama had validated me. My voice had been heard.

Two months later the phone rang. I looked at the incoming call, no name, just an unfamiliar number. I usually don't answer those calls because it's most likely a telemarketer on the other end, but this time something told me to pick up. A man gave me his name, the way telemarketers do and I confirmed he was in fact speaking to me. He identified himself as a member of the President's Committee for People with Intellectual Disabilities. President Obama had asked him to follow up on a letter sent him regarding my son. I felt a body rush of elation and nervousness simultaneously.

We chatted for the next thirty minutes about the need for a national conversation about autism, its aging population, and the need for a plan to care for them. I expressed my gratitude for President Obama's letter, and also for his phone call. I told him how much it meant to be validated and heard. Parents like me are not often heard. Our cries to meet the needs of our children are often dismissed or become an uphill battle of negotiation with agencies and schools. He praised my advocacy for my son and my volunteer work. He promised to send a follow-up email with his contact information should I have any additional questions. Days later I received that email as promised.

Unbeknownst to me, this would initiate an eight-month online email conversation that would spotlight a much bigger issue.

# THE POWER OF THE PEN

*Stay the course* became a mantra I would eat, breathe and sleep. Like a warrior, I picked up my pen and went into battle with my words. I had accumulated almost a year's worth of regular mail and emails documenting the vicious cycle of misinformation, unprofessionalism, and lack of support from both the local DDS office and the forced temporary day hab placement. Most important were the assessments by various board-certified behavioral clinicians, all reporting that Ian required 1:1 staff to support his high needs. Computer at hand, I spent day after day reviewing, printing and compiling emails and observation reports. The research alone was grueling. Re-reading each document forced me to relive the past year. I could feel my blood pressure rising one page at a time. I had to take breaks and walk away; these documents were literally making me ill.

Somehow, I managed to compile a timeline of the unfolding mayhem accompanied by an overview cover letter. I emailed a copy of that letter to the man I spoke to on the phone; Dr. J. The letter was addressed to the commissioner, his boss.

The only way to reach the commissioner was by regular US mail; no email address was available to the public. I printed out a hard copy, clipped the cover letter to the compiled data and slipped it into a large manila envelope. I stood in the post office experiencing a moment of both fear and surrender. I put it into the postal worker's hands, sending it by certified mail. In a few days, it would find its way to his desk in Washington, DC. The trajectory of my son's future was now in the hands of the powers that be.

*Dear Commissioner, I write to update you on the outcome of my son's day habilitation placement referenced in your letter of July 23, 2015. The assessment of my son's needs by the initial day hab resulted in a request for 1:1 staff support for Ian. This is the third day hab to call for 1:1 support for my son. Prior to this assessment, DDS local office denied 1:1 funding claiming it remained uncertain why a full time 1:1 was necessary for Ian's success, regardless of the detailed rationale for how it would be used.*

I went on to say that DDS stated funding must be allocated to where the needs are greatest and there simply isn't enough for everyone to have everything they want; that day hab staff ratios must be sufficient to provide the required support.

I continued, *this is not about what anyone wants, it's about what Ian needs and that he has a documented history of 1:1 support since preschool.* I continued to detail Ian's diagnosis of severe autism: below 40 IQ, mild mental retardation, severely limited receptive language, nonverbal, and prescribed multiple medications that require annual Rogers Law review.

*To date, three objective day hab assessments completed by qualified clinicians have all required 1:1 support for acceptance into their program. DDS sent their own behavior clinician to observe Ian. It is unclear why a fourth assessment would be necessary.*

*The current temporary placement was a forced placement due to no other options offered by DDS local office. My experience with the program has only reinforced my original impression of inexperienced, unprofessional staff. Two incidents have gone undocumented and unreported. DDS was informed of both.*

I went on to quote the program coordinator's input that appeared on Ian's Individual Service Program (ISP) which stated *"although Ian is verbal, he communicates using short phrases or single words. Ian was asked what he would like to accomplish while here at the day program. However, no suggestions were made at this time."'*

I went on to state in the letter that the Program's Safety Assessment, which asked multiple questions about what my son could and could not do, were inaccurately answered. For example, one question asked if my son could safely evacuate independently from his residence during an emergency in less than three minutes. I informed the Commissioner,

*The Program coordinator had checked "yes" but this was not only not true, but unsafe information about Ian. Of four pages of questions, eight were answered incorrectly, six needed clarification. Numerous statements in the ISP evaluations, including speech, OT, PT and nutritional assessments are also incorrect. I am enclosing remarks separate from this letter.*

*The ISP meeting was held in July 2015. To date, I have not received any follow up correspondence from DDS or the program.*

*Needless to say, I have little confidence in the staff at the program to care for my son and less in the information they are reporting. I began this process with DDS on 8/28/14 with the understanding this would provide ample time to search for an appropriate placement. I was also led to believe that DDS would assist me in this search. This has proven not to be the case.*

*Now, almost 13 months since I began this search, DDS still has*

*not provided any other day hab options. I continue to feel unsupported and challenged in trying to secure an appropriate placement for my son. If the current placement continues, I fear unwanted behaviors will increase and will minimize possibilities of his acceptance anywhere. As Ian's legal guardian I am responsible to make decisions in his best interest, but DDS provides the funding. Repeated requests for 1:1 are falling on deaf ears. My hands are tied.*

*This is not about pointing fingers. This is about demonstrating how difficult and sometimes frightening this process can be for a parent/guardian of an adult child with high needs like Ian. I am one of many trying to make decisions in the best interest of my child while navigating a system of rules and regulations with little assistance. Respectfully, ..."*

I enclosed all assessments and emails referenced in the letter.


FALL HAD ARRIVED ONCE AGAIN. Still no new programs to explore from the local DDS office, no effort on its part to help move Ian out of the nightmare placement forced upon him. The DDS local office held the purse strings to Ian's safety and future. But staff members were not invested in his best interest; they had their budget heads on.

They were trying to wear me down, blocking me at every turn, ignoring clinical behavioral data provided by outside day hab programs, all reflecting Ian's need of 1:1 support. The unspoken message was loud and clear: *DDS can't afford to fund a 1:1 staff person for Ian.* My response: *Ian's safety is at risk; we can't afford not to support him.*

I remained steadfast to keeping this search alive. I was walking a tightrope without a net, determined to reach the other side, never looking down.

October began with an email:

*Dear Johanne, Hope all is well for you and Ian. I just wanted to follow up to learn if there has been any improvement so far. Please let me know.*

*Thank you and Best Regards*

It was from Dr. J. What a pleasant surprise. Someone was still listening. I promptly responded:

*Thank you for checking in. I am disappointed to report there has been no progress. To date, the DDS local office has not offered any options. In fact, the recent Individual Support Plan states: "Another day habilitation program is being sought by Ian's guardian." This statement only reinforces DDS's continued nonsupport in my search for an appropriate day hab. The ISP will require revision due to incorrect and missing information. In addition, the goals and objectives for Aimwell Alliance are missing from the packet. The ISP meeting was in July and this paperwork was sent mid-September. In summary, I am concerned for Ian's safety and am at a loss about how to move forward. I welcome any assistance you can offer.*
*Thank you.*

Weeks quickly passed, the Paris attacks had just happened, the world was in crisis and I felt helpless knowing Ian was in an unsafe situation. My heart ached with despair. We had no choice but to wait. Each day I said a prayer, took a breath and kept faith this was moving in the right direction. My voice had been heard by President Obama. I was now connected to one of his people and needed to trust the process. Being in the moment, doing the work, focusing on what was in front of me, that is how I moved through my day. Every day I checked my email; every day I pulled in strength to get to the next step. It felt like crossing a desert, an endless horizon of sand and no oasis in sight.

Thanksgiving would soon be here and Christmas was right around the corner. Federal holidays translated into closed doors on schools and government agencies, further delay in response time. The wait continued.

# THE STRAW THAT BROKE THE CAMEL'S BACK

*I*n early December, I received an email from the Residential Manager of Ian's group home. As I read, my pulse quickened and my heart sank. There had been an incident in the van transporting my son to his day hab program. Ian experienced an SIB (self-injurious behavior) which was reported to have lasted approximately 20 minutes. The cause of the agitation was unknown. His Residential Manager brought Ian back to the group home where he could calm and ground him. He followed through with notifying me and filing a formal report, copying DDS local office. The local office continued to hold tight to its purse strings as Ian's safety was clearly at risk. The truth had surfaced once again; Ian needed 1:1 staff support.

I cringed. My son's life was crumbling before me as I was forced to watch helplessly from the sidelines. Life decisions were being made for my son by people who did not know him, by people who saw him as only a number, a dollar sign in a budget. He was left in the care of untrained staff who did not know how to handle his needs causing his frustrations to escalate. Each frustration reinjured the self-inflicted bump on his head. The hematoma got bigger and bigger and just as the bruises were healing, new ones appeared. The vicious cycle got worse each day.

Ian came home for a short visit at Christmas. The large bump protruded from the left side of his forehead. If I didn't know better I would have feared he had a tumor. Weeks later the injured tissue was still trying to heal, covered with red, brown and yellow skin. My desire to protect him was blocked by the powers that be; I felt indescribably helpless. I cringed at the thought that in a few days he would be forced to return to that dreadful day program. How frightening it must be for Ian to live in a world where he can't communicate his basic needs, to be in a position of total dependence, total vulnerability where he literally has no voice, no choice.

It was January, a new month, a new year, time to begin again. My fingers automatically began typing:

January 12, 2016

*Hi Dr. J, I just wanted to touch base regarding Ian's current situation. In November I was able locate two potential day habs for my son; both have openings and will observe him this month. Should he be accepted at either facility, my fear remains that funding will continue to be denied by the local DDS office if 1:1 support is required.*

I told Dr. J about the self-inflicted injury in the van.

*I have not been notified by the local office about the incident, nor have I received a copy of the incident report. Despite my efforts as his legal guardian, Ian remains in a precarious position. My hope is to change that as soon as possible so we don't continue to experience lost opportunities. I will keep you posted.*

To my surprise Dr. J replied that same day. He said he was sorry about the unfortunate incident and assured me it would be investigated. As I read the next few words on the screen, tears welled up in my eyes and ran down my face. He would contact the local office and ensure proper funding was available for 1:1 support.

Was this really happening? Was my son finally going to get the support he needed? I took a moment to digest what I had just read. It was a moment beyond words, beyond gratitude. The new year was now filled with hope for a brighter future, but more work still needed to be done. I needed to secure a day habilitation program that would support his needs. I rolled up my sleeves and went to work, searching online for programs near his group home. I cross referenced the locations on Google Maps to make sure they were within the required limit of 30-40 minute drive from his residence, collected phone numbers and dredged up my old cold-calling skills. There was no phone call or email from the local office, no guarantee yet that 1:1 funding was available. I kept the faith and continued my day hab search *as if* it was.

# CUSTER'S LAST STAND

*I* was able to find two day hab programs near Ian's group home; both had openings, an unexpected bonus. Most day habilitation programs are at capacity and have long waiting lists. The alarming rate of autism diagnosis alone would fill every slot available. Although both programs welcomed all disabilities, both were trained specific to autism.

Return to square one. Observation and assessment of Ian by each program to make sure he was a good fit. Visit the program and tour the facility and finally secure placement. The first program would observe Ian on February 3rd. Even though I now had two potential day habs close to Ian's group home, I was convinced this one was the one.

After observing Ian and sharing information about his needs, the Executive Director was optimistic that the program would be a good fit for him and wanted me to tour the facility. The tour was scheduled without hesitation; we would meet on the 9th, but Mother Nature had other plans. I was forced to cancel due to an unexpected snowstorm. The tour was quickly rescheduled for the following Friday.

It was an unusually sunny warm day for mid-February and great for traveling over the bridge. Accompanied by my friend Francine, my second pair of eyes and ears, we met with the Executive Director and two other staff members to discuss their program and my son's needs. The conversation quickly turned rigid and negative which left me confused. "So, you don't think your program is a good fit for my son?" I asked.

The director's reply was vague. "I'm not saying no, I will have to speak with his residential staff."

They had led me to believe this was a program that would support Ian's needs. What were they talking about? Why was I wasting my time if this was not an appropriate program for my son? Had I not provided enough information in the initial screening? I left feeling like I had traveled two hours under false pretense, false hope. I got back in the car, Francine took the wheel. I felt defeated and deceived.

Out of nowhere, a thought popped in my head to visit the other program. I did not have an appointment, but we were in the area and it was worth a phone call. I tapped the number into my cell phone. My contact there was out for the day, but I was told someone would get back to me. Now what? I felt stuck.

Within minutes the phone rang. One of the staff asked if I could tour the facility next week. I explained that I had traveled two hours to get here and asked if it would be possible to get a ten-minute tour while I was in the area. Without hesitation, he said, "Let me make a phone call and call you right back." Again, within minutes the phone rang. He could meet us in an hour. That gave us time to GPS the location and get some lunch.

The facility was spacious, clean and had a calm air about it. The layout was similar to my son's residential school and would certainly feel like home to him. The energy was light and positive; you could see it beaming from the faces of the individuals who attended the program as well as the staff. All appeared friendly and happy. Since this was an impromptu visit, I knew it was real.

Our tour included rooms for puzzles, cooking, eating and a sensory room for quiet time complete with a bean bag chair, yoga music and soft lights. Our guide was clearly passionate about his work and committed to helping adults with disabilities. He invited us to join him in his office. We discussed Ian's needs and he assured me they were familiar with individuals like my son and would like to set up an observation to put the process in motion. I did have one question, the deciding question, the one I was almost afraid to say out loud; was the local DDS office providing funding for 1:1 support? The answer came back a resounding yes! Relief and joy simultaneously filled my heart. The long search had finally ended. My gratitude meter blew off the charts!

My son is now placed and spending his days in this supportive setting; a place where he can be cared for in a safe, stimulating, creative environment that promotes life skills, social and personal growth. This is truly a gift.

As I look back to March 2015, when my son turned 22 and was forced into a temporary day habilitation placement, the neglect he endured, the denial after denial for funding from the DDS local office, I feel blessed that he landed safely on his feet. To say it was a challenging journey is an understatement. I am forever grateful to President Obama and his staff, specifically Dr. J, whose concern and compassion for Ian's situation changed the trajectory of his life.

In March 2016, Ian turned 23 years old, a birthday that not only celebrated another year, but one that marked a rebirth. We were reaping the rewards of persistence and fortitude. A mother's love for her child has given him life again, one with dignity and sense of belonging.

# LOOSE ENDS

*Surrender to what is.*

# FORGIVE ME

By 1998 Doug had remarried and divorced wife number four (I was number three) and moved on to his next girlfriend. Linda was a bleachblonde with long red nails and a North Jersey accent. I met her briefly during Doug's one-time visit to the Cape to see the children, a visit he piggybacked onto a business trip she had in Boston. Doug and Linda lived together in the house that was formerly my grandmother's. She quickly took over managing his financial affairs, an area that was not his strength. She provided child support checks and medical insurance reimbursements accurately and on a timely basis, for which I was grateful.

One night the phone rang and the voice on the other end was Linda. She never called. She told me Doug had suffered a heart attack. He had survived and was doing well, but she wanted to let me know. We chatted a few minutes as I listened to the details. I hung up in disbelief. Doug was only 50 years old.

My eyes filled with unexpected tears. Where did these emotions come from? Why was I crying for this man? Hadn't he forced my divorce by choosing alcohol over his family? Why was I not saying, "serves him right?"

I went into deep reflection in search of an answer. Maybe because at one time we had loved each other enough to create two children. Or maybe because even though our marriage had failed, at least we had tried to mend it. Or perhaps simply because he is human. Doug recovered and several years passed. He did not phone often to talk to our daughter, Marianne, but when he did, their conversations were brief and he'd always end up chatting with me. Once he asked, "Do you forgive me, Jo?"

Without skipping a beat, I responded "yes." I knew in my heart it was true. I did not condone his behavior, but after two years of processing my feelings, I no longer harbored any anger toward him. Yes, I truly forgave him.

It must have taken a lot of courage for him to ask that question. I realized in that moment the Doug I knew had returned: he was genuine and spoke from the heart. A reminder that part of the man I had married somehow survived deep beneath the years of wreckage that had piled up around us. A reminder I had grown as a person. A stronger sense of resilience was added to my emotional toolbox that day, a tool that would be used regularly as the journey continued.

# THE SWINGS, A HAUNTING UNEXPECTED LESSON

*I*n early October 2012, eleven o'clock at night, the phone rang. My daughter was completely distraught. "Mom, Little Dougy called."

"What's the matter?" I said.

"Dad died," she replied, sobbing.

I was shocked. He had just turned 60. I went into take-charge mode and remained calm. My daughter was calling from her apartment. There was nothing I could do but talk her through it and handle the details in the morning.

In the blink of an eye, morning arrived and I was catapulted into autopilot. I quickly arranged bus tickets to NYC. The memorial service would take place across the Hudson River in a small town in New Jersey, her father's old stomping grounds, where he grew up and had been a police officer since he was eighteen, only a kid himself. We shopped for appropriate funeral wear, though I chose not to attend the service. Knowing he had been married five times and living with various girlfriends in between, I was sure I wouldn't be missed. After our divorce, he would always joke with me about his funeral. He said it would be like a scene from a Bette Midler movie where all the wives show up; then we'd share a good laugh. Now that scene could possibly play out.

Deep inside I also knew I would probably not be welcomed by his family and friends, and that my daughter needed to meet them on common ground without me. She had a chance at acceptance. She had not been seen by this side of the family since the age of four, when her father and I went our separate ways and the kids and I moved to Massachusetts.

Oddly enough, this man who had just passed, my ex-husband, and the ex-husband of others, brought my own bag of mixed feelings to the surface. I remembered him clearly choosing alcohol over his family, which sealed my decision for divorce. I remembered being very sad and distraught over losing this idea of family, the white picket fence, an all-American scene from a Norman Rockwell painting. My sadness turned to anger, but finally, I was able to forgive him. Not forget, but forgive, forgive us and move on. I remembered him talking to me once about a medical issue. At the time, he had been living with a woman for about two years, whom I liked and developed a good relationship with. "Why don't you talk to her about it?" I remembered asking him.

"I can't tell her things like that, Jo, she doesn't understand; you understand," he replied.

It spoke volumes about our connection, even at that point. Thoughts and emotions emerged that had been buried deep inside and needed to be released.

When we reached New Jersey, I ordered flowers online to be sent to the service and struggled with the cards. Cards plural; I made sure there were two arrangements, one from the kids and one from me. They needed to be separate; it was my closure, wishing his spirit peace and serenity.

When the order was complete, I broke down in tears. No one even thought to ask how I felt about his death. No one thought I might be experiencing a sense of loss. It even surprised me on some level, but why? I suppose having two children with this man was bond enough, one that could never be broken. I lost him to the bottle, lost him as a husband and as a father. Now I allowed myself to grieve and feel yet another loss, the loss of life itself.

Upon our return home, my daughter still needed to process all that had occurred. I spent hours showing her old photos and telling stories about her father. Some were funny, some sad, and some not so nice, but all were true. I gave her the gold heart locket he gave to me on the first Valentine's Day before she was born, inscribed "love Doug" with the date. I also gave her my wedding band; its three thin bands of different color gold, rose, yellow and white. The bands are intertwined and cannot be separated. I told her it was symbolic of how we began our marriage. I was two months pregnant with her at the time, so we began our journey as three.

A few years after his death, the house where we lived and where he died was put on the market. My daughter found it online. Curious to take a look, we sat together in front of my computer screen to take a virtual tour. I had memories of my own childhood from frequent Sunday visits to grandma's house. So, we reminisced about the rooms and how they were changed and the "remember when's" started to flow.

The last picture was a view of the backyard. The swing set was still there, the one I bought at a garage sale for $20. There it stood, this old aluminum swing set, after twenty years. He never took it down. He had no other children to play on it, and yet it remained intact. Why? I was speechless.

The stark black and white image of empty swings seemed symbolic. Without words it spoke about our children, our relationship, a family that once was and the boundless connecting energy we have to one another through the blood of our children.

# CONNECTING THE DOTS

*I*n 2005, Steve Jobs delivered a commencement speech at Stanford University. He spoke about how you can only connect the dots in life as you look backwards and the importance of trusting the dots will connect in your future.

Looking back, it's clear each choice I made led me to another dot connecting a way through this journey. I reached out to many who helped me along the way and some who didn't, but it was the force within that moved me forward. I did not have the knowledge, the experience or the confidence to do what I was doing, but I did have faith. I did it with compassion, I did it with courage, and I did it with commitment. I moved forward from the inside out, one step at a time and trusted I was being led in the right direction.

Each day I reached into the depths of my soul to pull out another ounce of strength, another ounce of courage, another ounce of wisdom I didn't know existed that launched me into possibilities I never imagined.

# CONNECTING MORE DOTS

*S*ince the beginning of Ian's public school career, occupational therapy was a part of his special needs program; that program always included a swing. There were all types of therapy swings, platform swings, slings for snug pressure and barrel swings, to name a few; all contributing to sensory integration to regulate the body's emotional and physical senses.

For Ian, the swing helped integrate his body space awareness while suspended in motion, producing a state of grounded calm. In a word, it was healing. Perhaps the original swing set still standing in the backyard of my grandmother's house is also healing. It stood as a reminder of the family that once was and the letting go of the one that could have been.

# A GRATITUDE CHECK FROM WOODY

*I* was in the midst of reading Creativity, Inc., by Ed Catmull, a book detailing the history and creative process of Pixar Animation Studios when this quote appeared: "I can't stop Andy from growing up, but I wouldn't miss it for the world." Catmull is quoting Woody, the toy cowboy character from the movie *Toy Story 2*. In the movie, the boy Andy was growing up, soon to leave his childhood behind, including his cowboy friend. The quote caught me off guard. My eyes filled with tears.

My son's growing years flashed through my mind's eye; the day the doctor diagnosed him with autism, watching him through a one-way mirror working with therapists, and leaving him at his residential school for the very first time, letting go. I thought about the day-to-day challenges autism presented and how our lives were shaped by trying to meet those needs. Autism changed the way we lived, worked and played as a family. Even when Ian triumphed, another challenge would soon be before us; each success was just a plateau, a resting place to regroup before continuing on the long road ahead. Ian is now a young man and although we have made progress along the way, we are still on that road, a road that will last for his lifetime and beyond mine.

Like most aging parents in my shoes, I am running a desperate race against time. Left no choice, I must navigate systems and agencies, hoping to secure Ian's future care, for the time when I will no longer be there to manage my son's affairs. As we continue along this journey, despite the challenges, I am grateful for Woody's innocent voice as it reminds me:

I can't stop Ian from growing up, but I wouldn't have missed it for the world.

# RESILIENCE, IS IT LEARNED THROUGH ADVERSITY?

*R*esilience is *"an ability to recover,"* according to Merriam-Webster's dictionary. Some psychologists say optimism, positive attitude and the ability to manage one's emotions may contribute to a person's resilience. Research studies continue to ask the question, is this learned or innate? I'm not sure. I am by nature an optimist; although I have been flooded with many emotions that may not always be categorized as manageable.

As a kid, I learned to make do with what I had and never felt deprived. Even though the kids across the street had Oreo cookies, it was okay that we had the wanna-be store brand; we were grateful for it. Other kids had fancy store-bought skateboards; my dad made them for us. Naturally, we thought we had the coolest ones on the block! It was a matter of perception. As I grew into adulthood, I spent the better half of the 70's and most of the 80's focused on survival; a balancing act of trying to climb the corporate ladder during the day, working toward my bachelor's degree at night, fighting for equal pay and dodging sexual harassment along the way. A cascade of changes spontaneously unfolded; job changes, moving from apartment to apartment, relationships came and went; all building blocks to adaptation, to resilience. By the time I experienced the attempted abduction, my instinct launched me into action, not fear. Not that fear didn't exist; there just wasn't time to think about it. A voice that lived in my head always appeared with an alternate approach, although it did take me quite a while to let go of the scenario of happiness equals family with the white picket fence; I really wanted that to be true.

Maturity and the reality that I had choices along the way became more and more apparent after becoming a mother of two, responsible for their vulnerable young lives, not just my own. Through the challenges of autism, single parenting and just plain surviving, there were many times I felt I had no choice but to make a choice. Sometimes the choice was to do nothing at all, but it was still a choice. I came to realize it's not about what you're capable of, it's about what you are willing to do, what you are willing to risk to make that choice a reality.

# REFLECTION

*a*utism changes everything. It teaches you to see life through a different lens and alters your way of living, your way of thinking. Through living with this unpredictable, demanding condition and rising to meet its challenges, I've learned that even the smallest step forward can be the most rewarding and that a momentous achievement doesn't change reality; there is still no cure. Choices were made and there's no going back; surrender to what is. My dreams were broken, but not my spirit; more choices are to be made ahead. Perhaps the choice to begin is the most important of all. Consequences in life can be good or bad, but in the end, it's all a choice.

# NOTE FROM THE AUTHOR

I took a picture of a paperweight and posted it on Facebook one night after putting the finishing touches on the first draft of this book. The paperweight was given to me as a gift, it's a small replica of the Wicked Witch of the East legs with striped stockings and the magical ruby slippers Dorothy ended up wearing in the movie *The Wizard of Oz*. Finishing the first draft was a huge accomplishment and the shoes were a whimsical way to send a message out to the universe: *I'm ready to click my heels and escape to some well-deserved down time!* My post said "Anybody know where I can get a pair of these?"

One response in particular caused me to pause. A friend simply said,

"I think you have a pair."

*Wow*, I thought, *she's right, I do have a pair.* The magic metaphor of these ruby-red shoes had touched my life. Looking back over more than twenty years, the path I was kicked on, the challenges, the choices and the courage to move forward in the uncertainty of it all, was shrouded in a protective bubble guided by a Good Witch of the North energy. Even in what appeared to be the darkest, most wicked moments, I was able not only to move through, but move forward. In the end, I landed on my feet, with a new beginning that allowed me to share what I had learned. I had not only survived this leg of my journey, but realized through the process I had transformed our lives. We made it over the rainbow.

# EPILOGUE

This book is not meant to point fingers, cast blame or suggest everyone write a letter to the President - but rather, to **Begin a Conversation**. To spark meaningful discussion and ignite new thinking that bridges the gap between public school education and long-term care for adults with special needs.

When my son was born in 1993, 1 in 150 were diagnosed with autism nationwide. When I began writing this story in 2015, the rate of Autism diagnosis had climbed to 1 in 68. As I publish this book, in 2018 the Center for Disease Control released a startling new statistic: Autism diagnosis is now 1 in 59.

By sharing my personal story, I hope to inspire others and let them know their voices matter; they have a choice. We have a responsibility to continue to speak for those unable to speak for themselves. To share stories that educate and empower; to lead by example.

**Let's keep the conversation going!**

# ACKNOWLEDGMENTS

I cannot begin to thank the many teachers and support staff, doctors and nurses, friends and family, therapists and nonprofit organizations that helped along this journey. I especially want to acknowledge those who choose to work with special needs children and adults; your choice makes a monumental difference in our children and their families' lives and for that I am eternally grateful.

President Obama, thank you sir, for taking the time to answer my letter. Your simple acknowledgement set into motion possibilities that changed the trajectory of my son's life.

My heartfelt thanks to Habitat for Humanity and all those who swung a hammer to make my home possible. Habitat doesn't just build houses, it builds communities and changes lives.

Thank you, Rose Connors, for staying the course and working as hard as I did to see this story through to completion. Your guidance and seasoned editing skills gave my story a clear, strong voice.

Thank you, Kate Conway, for your creative eye, endless patience with my questions and guiding me through the nuts and bolts of publishing.

Dan and Joyce Miller, thank you for your copyright expertise and supportive advice. You truly are The Copyright Detectives.

I also want to thank my friends: Nicky who encouraged me to tell this story and Jan who has been a guiding light during times when I thought all was lost.

I am forever indebted to my parents who allowed me to descend upon them with two kids and a dog only a few short years into their retirement on Cape Cod.

Most of all I want to thank my children, for giving me reason to get up every morning and find the courage to move forward through each day.

# CREDITS

A special thank you to the following who generously allowed permission for their quotes to appear in this story.

TAXI DRIVER

© 1976, 2004 Columbia Pictures Industries, Inc.

All Rights Reserved

Courtesy of Columbia Pictures

The Untamed Tongue by Thomas Szasz, Copyright 1990 by Open Court Publishing. Reprinted by permission of Open Court Publishing.

## Additional Credits

Rogers Law Guide

https://www.mass.gov/files/documents/2016/08/wx/rogers-guardianship-booklet.pdf

Apollo 13 "Houston, we've got a problem."

EP-76, Produced by the Office of Public Affairs National Aeronautics and Space Administration,

Washington, DC 20546 US GOVERNMENT PRINTING OFFICE, 1970 384-459

NOTE: No Longer In Print

pdf version by Jerry Woodfill of the Automation, Robotics, and Simulation Division,

Johnson Space Center, Houston, Texas 77058

# ABOUT THE AUTHOR

Johanne is a writer, autism advocate and mother of a son with severe autism. Through sharing her personal story, she hopes to raise awareness of this growing diagnosis and the need to bridge the gap between public education and adult services. Most of all, she hopes it inspires others to find fortitude and faith within themselves and know that their voice matters. She continues to work with special needs students in the public-school system and live in her Habitat for Humanity Home on Cape Cod.

Made in United States
Orlando, FL
25 March 2022